# The Passionate Philosopher

Margaret Crosland was one of the first
people in Britain to translate the writings of
the Marquis de Sade and is now an
acknowledged authority on his life and work.
Her translations of stories by Sade, *The
Mystified Magistrate* and *The Gothic Tales of the
Marquis de Sade*, are both available from
Peter Owen. She has also written
biographies of Colette, Cocteau and Edith
Piaf, as well as translating literature from
French and Italian, and she has published
studies of British and French women
novelists. Her most recent biography, *Simone
de Beauvoir* (herself a perceptive analyst of
Sade), was published to great acclaim by
Heinemann in 1992. She lives in Sussex.

# The
# Passionate Philosopher

## A Marquis de Sade Reader

*Selected and translated from the French by*
MARGARET CROSLAND

Minerva

**A Minerva Paperback**
THE PASSIONATE PHILOSOPHER

First published in Great Britain 1991
by Peter Owen Publishers
This Minerva edition published 1993
by Mandarin Paperbacks
an imprint of Reed Consumer Books Ltd
Michelin House, 81 Fulham Road, London SW3 6RB
and Auckland, Melbourne, Singapore and Toronto

This edition and translations herein
copyright © Margaret Crosland 1991

A CIP catalogue record for this title
is available from the British Library
ISBN 0 7493 9088 3

Printed and bound in Great Britain
by Cox & Wyman Ltd, Reading, Berks

# Contents

*Conjectural portrait of de Sade*

# Introduction

Four major novels, many short stories, dialogues, plays, pamphlets, letters, journals – not counting minor and still unpublished works – plus a legacy to language and an unenviable reputation for near-criminal behaviour and pornography: all this identifies the Marquis de Sade, possibly the most talked about of unread authors in or out of France, his home country. Few writers have excited so much controversy or left so many problems, biographical, social and literary, many still unresolved after some two hundred years. The poet Apollinaire called him 'the freest spirit who ever lived'.

Who was this man? How did he live and come to earn his alarming reputation? What is the relationship between mythology and fact?

The extraordinary writer whose name has passed into dictionaries and reference books world-wide, Donatien-Alphonse-François de Sade, was born in Paris in 1740 in the Hôtel de Condé, on the Left Bank, later demolished to make way for the well-known Théâtre de l'Odéon. His family background was grand: the writer's father, the Comte de Sade, spent his life in the army and the diplomatic service, while his marriage brought him a distant alliance to the younger branch of the Bourbons, the ruling dynasty in France. The de Sade family, whose genealogy can be traced back to the Middle Ages, was of Provençal origin and had included several lawyers and many clerics. One early member, Laure de Sade, had been Petrarch's adored if elusive Laura, first seen by the poet in Avignon in 1327.

Donatien-Alphonse-François was to grow up as an only child, an elder sister having died at the age of two and a younger one surviving only a few days. He did not see a great deal of his mother, who was lady-in-waiting to the Princesse de Condé, while his grandmother in Provence was so over-affectionate and indulgent that the little boy was allowed to become vain and violent. He later admitted as much. Four aunts who had entered the religious life also spoilt him, the only surviving boy of his generation. His education followed the usual pattern adopted by the French aristocracy at the time. Between the ages of four and ten he was educated mainly by his uncle, a worldly abbé who lived partly at one of the family properties, Saumane, and partly at the Cistercian Abbaye d'Ebreuil, near Limoges in central France.

The abbé, like many of his contemporaries, was hardly a model character. Admittedly he wrote a biography of the family's best-known ancestor, Laure de Sade, but the religious life did not concern him greatly. Two mistresses, a mother and her daughter, lived openly in his house, and he frequented the establishment of a procuress. Unfortunately for him, one of his visits coincided with a police raid and the abbé was sent to prison for a time. His nephew was surely too young to react personally to this behaviour but he no doubt grew up assuming it to be normal. And up to a point, it was.

However, at ten the boy was old enough for serious education and was sent back to Paris to attend the Lycée Louis-le-Grand which was directed, under strict discipline, by Jesuits. Sade seems to have appreciated the tutor allotted to him, the Abbé Amblet, with whom he remained in touch for many years, and at the Lycée he had his first experience of acting in and producing plays. However, his regular education was over after four years, for at fourteen the schoolboy was old enough to join the army. Since he was a member of an old and aristocratic family, he was able to join the Light Horse, one of the King's favourite regiments. The marquis spent altogether seventeen years in the army, becoming a sub-lieutenant in the King's infantry regiment, then a cornet in the Carabinier regiment (which took part in the Seven Years War), next a captain in a cavalry regiment and finally maître de camp. When he was only twenty, in 1764, Sade acquired more responsibility when his father passed over to him the lieutenant-generalcy of four provinces: Bresse, Bugey, Valromey and Gex.

Army life, much of it spent in Germany, brought the young officer his first experiences with girls, and as soon as he was back in Paris he had even more choice of companions, all flattered by the attentions of a young officer generous with money and eager for entertainment. Girls, betting, laziness: his behaviour upset his father and in fact Sade was hardly satisfied with himself. He wrote out his thoughts to the Abbé Amblet, aware that so far he had not developed any good relationship with a woman: 'Could I imagine that the girls whom I saw could truly bring me pleasure? Alas, does one ever really enjoy happiness that is bought, and can love without delicacy ever be really affectionate? My *amour propre* is hurt now at the thought that I was loved only because I probably paid better than the next man.' The Comte de Sade, whom his son described as 'the most affectionate of fathers', was not pleased when he had to pay the marquis's gambling debts and listen to complaints about his behaviour, especially his passion for entertainment. The count, who was somewhat austere by nature and consumed by perpetual money worries, admitted that his son's 'little heart or rather body is wildly combustible': surely it was time to arrange a marriage for him, then he might settle down.

Sade himself was beginning to think about marriage, but in a romantic, unrealistic way, for he had fallen in love. He had met a girl who was a year younger than himself and like him came of an old Provençal family. Her name was Laure de Lauris, and Sade, addressing her as *ma chère amie, ma divine amie*, 'sole support of my heart, sole delight of my life', wrote a long and passionate letter to her. His father had already chosen a bride for him, as was usual, *de rigueur* in fact, at the time, but Sade told Laure that he would not marry this other girl. The Comte de Sade had almost given up hope for his son, finding him intractable in everything, but in this case he had encountered an unexpected ally. Laure refused to marry the marquis; she had set her heart on someone else. For the first time in his life the marquis had to do what he was told. Like his near-contemporary Edward Gibbon he sighed as a lover and obeyed as a son. He submitted to the arranged marriage and in 1763 Renée-Pélagie de Montreuil became Marquise de Sade.

The count must have been highly relieved. The Président de Montreuil was a successful lawyer who had made money and the family seemed to be so well inclined towards their new in-laws that the count felt guilty about introducing his difficult son to them. Yet father and son both needed the wealthy Montreuils, since the count had even had to borrow money to outfit his domestic staff for the entertainment and ceremonies incurred by the marriage.

Sade was twenty-three when he entered into this loveless but useful arrangement and, if his elders had hoped he would settle down, he did not do so. Five months after the wedding he left the Montreuils' Normandy château on some pretext and in Paris took a girl named Jeanne Testard, who made fans, into a small house near the rue Mouffetard and locked her into a bedroom with him. He wanted not only sex with flagellation but sex with blasphemous acts. The terrified girl co-operated only to save her life, she said, for her seducer threatened her with pistols and a sword. Later, after the girl had understandably complained to the police, Sade was arrested, and after cross-examination he found himself imprisoned in the *donjon* of Vincennes, a forbidding fortress built in the Middle Ages. The King had signed the necessary documents authorizing his punishment.

The marquis affected to repent, his desperate father exerted influence at court and after a few weeks the prisoner was released, subject to certain conditions. He was to be a prisoner not of the State but of his in-laws. He was to live with them at the Château d'Echauffour where a resident police inspector would also keep an eye on him.

But Sade's true gaoler was his mother-in-law, Madame de Montreuil. She had already paid off the girl, Jeanne Testard, hoping for her silence, and began to wonder how she could keep this young man in control: at all costs his behaviour must not compromise her family ambitions. She referred to him as *un drôle d'enfant*, 'an odd child'. The phrase sounds dismissive, but it may disguise the fact that Madame de Montreuil, who spent her life in social climbing and intrigue, was attracted to the marquis herself. She was as well known for her charm as for her powers of persuasion and in her the young man met his match. In their different ways, they both liked to dominate and spent their lives looking for ways of doing so.

Was Donatien-Armand-François an attractive man? He is never described as handsome, and the only authentic likeness to have survived shows him as an adolescent. Yet he must have possessed a kind of charisma, a dynamism that some women could not resist. The police reports are more informative than personal recollections: he was about five feet five inches tall, his face pale and pock-marked, his hair a light chestnut in colour, his eyes blue, his gaze intense.

Fascinating or not as a man, everything he did seemed acceptable to his wife: either she was in love with him or she was cold, indifferent. Sade was indifferent about nothing, and where his private pleasures were concerned he was devious and determined. When he believed he had shown sufficient repentance after the

Jeanne Testard affair he began to spend time in Paris again, haunting the theatres and the Opéra, where there was no shortage of attractive young actresses and dancers. He seems to have been genuinely in love with Mademoiselle Colet, who was eighteen when he first met her. She was officially kept by the Marquis de Lignerai,* who was apparently ready to retire in favour of his rival. But Sade could not afford the girl. He even confessed his problem to Madame de Montreuil, who referred to his feelings as *une frénésie*. Like every upper- or middle-class eighteenth-century mother-in-law she did not expect marital fidelity but she hoped the young man would at least maintain a show of discretion.

He did not, and was soon infatuated with Mademoiselle de Beauvoisin, a senior actress-courtesan aged twenty-two, and his behaviour with her was anything but discreet. He took her to the family château at La Coste in Provence, where he had the private theatre restored so that they could act together, assisted by professionals whom he called in, and by any available amateurs. The marquis also wrote plays for performance here. The young Beauvoisin was sometimes even presented as the marquise, or mistaken for her, but when she was at La Coste Renée-Pélagie would take part in the entertainments herself. She may well have believed that by this method she had more chance of keeping her husband's friendship, if nothing more, rather than through any jealous scenes.

Early in 1767 the Comte de Sade died suddenly. His son was emotionally upset by the loss and Madame de Montreuil was touched by his reaction. Was the young man, *le drôle d'enfant*, truly capable of family feeling? He could now have taken the style of comte, but apparently he preferred to be known almost always as marquis. That same year, late in August, his eldest son, Louis-Marie, was born, and everyone, including the two grandmothers, was pleased. When the Prince de Condé and the Princesse de Conti agreed to be godparents, Madame de Montreuil may have felt that her social ambitions were on the way to fulfilment.

---

* The name Lignerai is so spelt in a police report of 1764 quoted by the defence when Sade's publisher Pauvert was in the dock for obscenity in 1965. Sade's French biographer Gilbert Lély uses the same spelling.

However, there was no new chapter of happy domestic life. Sade was not satisfied with the minor dramas of the entertainment world and backstage theatre life. He wanted something more. It was on Easter Sunday 1768 that he saw Rose Keller, a thirty-six-year-old widow of German origin, begging in the place des Victoires. He took her to his little house at Arcueil, a place he kept, like most young aristocrats of the time, for sexual assignments, but merely told her he needed a chambermaid. Rose Keller foreshadowed Justine, the marquis's future and best-known downtrodden heroine. He made her undress, tied her down on a bed and beat her, using alternately a rod and a 'martinet', a whip with knotted cords, occasionally putting wax on her wounds, until he experienced orgasm. He then told her to wash, gave her some eau-de-vie for the wounds and plied her with boiled beef and wine. Afterwards he locked her in a bedroom, from which she escaped through the window and down a rope of knotted sheets. Sade's valet ran after her and offered her money, which she refused.

Naturally she complained. Within three days the local judge was listening to witnesses and by the fourth the Marquise de Montreuil was again paying hush-money to the victim.

However inexcusable the incident, Sade was by no means the only 'sadist' in mid-eighteenth-century France, or in the England of Sir Francis Dashwood's Hell-fire Club. Many members of the French aristocracy and even the King's brother, the Comte de Charolais, committed cruel sexual offences just as or even more serious, but, through family privilege and fortune, they escaped punishment. Sade did not escape entirely, neither he nor even his parents-in-law were powerful or rich enough for that, and he was made into something of a scapegoat, for his case was investigated by the criminal council of the Parlement de Paris, the highest court in the country. By the end of April the young man – he was still only twenty-eight – was sent briefly to the Château de Saumur, then to the gloomy fortress of Pierre-Encise, near Lyon, and from there to the Conciergerie in Paris. Yet again, through the intervention of his own mother and his mother-in-law, Sade did not suffer too much, for by November 1768 he was free.

He apparently did not wish to be free of his family, and his wife, although she did not know of all his misdeeds, forgave him what she did know. A second son, Donatien-Claude-Armand, was born in the summer of 1769, which, it transpired, was to be the most uneventful year in Sade's life. Even the police inspector who still kept him under observation, could find nothing to report. The marquis, interested in most aspects of culture, went to Holland to look at paintings and spent some time writing poetry, having 'borrowed the brush of Aretino'. His ambitious mother-in-law hoped he would appear at court, but unfortunately the King did not wish to see him there. He was prepared to return to the army, but again he did not seem popular, for the officers in charge of the Bourgogne Cavalerie regiment did not wish his presence either. He apparently visited London in 1770, carrying out some historical research, which he enjoyed. The Prince de Condé helped him to acquire a commission as maître de cavalerie, equivalent to the rank of colonel; but alas, the post was unpaid.

The year 1771 brought the birth of his daughter, Madeleine-Laure, but it ended the short period of peaceful existence for Sade, for that year he was back in prison, not for sexual offences but for a mundane question of debt. Sade was good at spending money, but like his father he was not good at collecting or managing the money that could have been brought in from the Château de La Coste. Even after selling his army commission he was still short of funds, his debtors would not wait and he was forced to spend a few weeks in the prison of Fort l'Evêque, near Lyon. However, he was able to leave in the autumn, having pledged to settle his debts. Sade then joined his family at La Coste, with its forty-two well-appointed rooms, which included his own library stocked with a wide range of books: classical authors, Pascal, Bossuet, the *romans libres* so fashionable at the time, and controversial books by such free-thinking authors as Baron d'Holbach.

But he could not limit himself to reading, however adventurous the books. At thirty-two he still felt compelled to go on acting out the fantasies which could not be satisfied either with his wife or with his favourite actress companions. During the early months of 1772 there was a different atmosphere about La Coste, owing to the arrival of a visitor from the Montreuil family, Anne-Prospère, one of Renée-Pélagie's younger sisters and her mother's favourite. It is not known why no husband had yet been found for her, or why she was a canoness, in other words a nun who had not yet taken her vows and was still living a privileged and worldly existence. Money had talked; the girl lived in a convent to which only noble families were normally admitted. Anne-Prospère was obviously attractive and intelligent. Sade's uncle, the abbé, apparently fell in love with her. So did Sade himself, and soon she was his mistress. Seducing a nun, however co-operative, was apparently even more exciting than beating a widow on Easter Sunday.

If Renée-Pélagie was secretly jealous of her sister, she continued to play the role of faithful wife, and a curious form of *ménage à trois* developed, the abbé wishing he could join in.

However, Sade still wanted something more, for intellectual discussions with a woman of his own class, even accompanied by a sexual relationship, were not enough. He needed women he could dominate in a crude physical way; he needed a short-term irresponsible escape from the conventional life of the château. At the end of June in 1772, on the pretext of attending to some financial business, he went to Marseille with his valet Latour and sent him in search of girls who were to join them in an orgy. Found through a procuress they were brought to the marquis, who offered them some sweets. Later the girls complained of feeling ill, and blamed the sweets, but not before they had accepted invitations to join in sexual intercourse with brutal accompaniments. Sometimes the girls were asked to whip the marquis, sometimes he whipped them, and Latour took part in the proceedings. As for the sweets, they were not poisoned but contained cantharides or 'Spanish fly', a well-known aphrodisiac much used at the time.

Like Rose Keller, the girls complained and in early July the arrest of Sade and Latour was ordered.

What was to be done? The marquis decided to leave France, but he would not leave alone. Latour must obviously go with him, and he took a second companion: Anne-Prospère. As for Renée-Pélagie, she did not complain, doing all she could to help the trio make a rapid escape. They went to Italy. Sade and Latour were accused in Marseille of 'poisoning and sodomy' and in September the Parlement at Aix condemned them to death, in their absence. On 12th September their effigies were publicly burnt in the centre of the town.

The years 1772–8 were so eventful in Sade's life that his adventures during that time read like fiction. Later in 1772 he left Italy, avoiding France and going to Savoy, which at that date was still part of Sardinia. But he was not safe even there, for he had underestimated Madame de Montreuil, infuriated by the seduction of her favourite daughter, even though Anne-Prospère had returned to France in November. The revengeful mother-in-law now arranged indirectly, through various diplomats, French and Sardinian, for Sade to be imprisoned, by order of King Charles-Emmanuel III of Sardinia, in the fortress of Miolans near Chambéry. His valet went with him and there they remained for nearly six months. In the spring of 1773 they escaped and the marquis returned to La Coste, convinced that his wife would continue to forgive him and help to conceal him.

Despite the searches by the police, and at least one raid on the château, Sade remained free for the whole of 1774 and half of the following year. His wife was apparently so devoted in her strange way that she had even taken legal action against her mother in an attempt to stop her interference. She did not succeed. Unfortunately too there was soon more for her to forgive. If Sade's feelings for Mademoiselle Colet a few years earlier had merited the description of 'frenzy', the direction of his 'frenzy' had long since turned away from 'love' into something totally destructive. If the orgy in Marseille had taken place on the premises of one of the girls involved, there now followed a whole series of orgies conducted in his own château. Some of the girls had been procured by a priest; boys took part also and so, apparently, did the Marquise de Sade herself. Perhaps these events were a trial run in some ways for those that formed *Les Cent Vingt Journées de Sodome*, Sade's first full-length book, although the château in which it was set was barricaded against the outside world. This was not the case at La Coste. The scandalous news spread to the surrounding villages, and later one angry father even tried to shoot the marquis.

Sade was soon a fugitive again, for Madame de Montreuil had now obtained the French king's permission for his arrest and the seizure of his papers. Once more he fled to Italy, where he stayed until the following year, collecting material for a book he was hoping to write about the country.

For six months or so in late 1776, back in France, he remained free, but early the following year he heard that his mother in Paris was ill. He decided that he would go to see her, but after a slow journey with his family he reached the city too late. The countess was dead. He was not too late for Madame de Montreuil's revenge: hearing of his presence she arranged at once to have him arrested under a *lettre de cachet*, an autocratic system that sanctioned imprisonment without trial. On 13th February he was taken once again to the *donjon* of Vincennes. There he began to plead with his mother-in-law for release and, on 6th March 1777, wrote in desperation to his wife: 'Get me out of this place, my dear wife, get me out, I beg you, for I feel I am dying by inches . . . love me in proportion to my sufferings, I ask no more, and believe me, I am in the depths of despair.'

He was not dying yet; he was to live another thirty-seven years. In June 1778 he was allowed out of Vincennes under escort to appear in court at Aix and appeal against the earlier death sentence following the Marseille affair. He was successful, escaping with a severe admonishment for *débauche outrée*. But he wanted total liberty. On the way back to Vincennes he escaped from his escort at Valence and yet again made his way back to La Coste. He was discovered, rearrested – for the *lettre de cachet* was still in force – and taken back to Vincennes.

What next? The authorities and Madame de Montreuil had had enough. Her social ambitions were thwarted, for in view of her son-in-law's behaviour, how could she marry off her remaining daughters? Sade was not allowed to see his wife for three years and was forced to spend most of his energy writing to her for supplies. He had nothing. The extravagant, hot-headed aristocrat faced a lonely, empty existence. But he was determined to fill it. His active physical life was over, but a new life began – a life of writing.

The extracts from writings by Sade in this anthology have been translated or summarized from the following editions of his work, all published in Paris unless otherwise stated:

*Aline et Valcour* (Brussels: J.J. Gay, 1822; *L'Oeuvre du Marquis de Sade* (*Les Maîtres de l'Amour*, 1909); *Les Crimes de l'Amour: Historiettes, Contes et Fabliaux* (Sagittaire, 1950); *Histoire Secrète d'Isabelle de Bavière* (Gallimard, 1953); *L'Affaire Pauvert* (Pauvert, 1957); *Histoire de Sainville et de Léonore* (from *Aline et Valcour*), ed. Gilbert Lély (Union Générale d'Editions, 1963); *Journal Inédit* (Gallimard, 1970); *La Philosophie dans le Boudoir* (Gallimard, 1976); *Oeuvres Complètes du Marquis de Sade* (Pauvert, 1986– ).

In the interests of clarity and readability, some of the original punctuation has been modified. The writer's erratic use of capital initials has also been brought into line.

MARGARET CROSLAND

*The Passionate Philosopher*

# Dialogue entre un Prêtre et un Moribond

The prisoner who had been in Vincennes since the early autumn of 1777 did not look round his cell one day and suddenly take up his pen in an onset of desperate frustration. He was already a writing man who had composed poetry (not very good, apparently, to judge from quotations) and plays, some of them produced during the private theatricals at La Coste. He wrote endless letters, many of which have survived, and kept a journal, which was burnt after his death. He continued to write plays and by mid-July 1782 he had completed a piece that is now fairly well known, first published in France in 1926 with a foreword by the Sade scholar Maurice Heine. This is the *Dialogue entre un Prêtre et un Moribond* (Dialogue between a Priest and a Dying Man).

The dialogue form was fashionable in eighteenth-century France, much used by Fontenelle and Diderot, and popular with Sade, who obviously relished its quasi-theatrical aspect. Speaking through the dying man the author uses the method of special pleading – he called it logic – which he developed all his life: he explains and attempts to justify his theories concerning 'nature' and 'reason', expressing his atheistic, anti-clerical beliefs in a style that seems fairly moderate when compared with some of his later exaggerations on the same theme. Sade presumably hoped to prove his powers of persuasion, for the priest joins the dying man in a last few hours of sensual pleasure, the nature of which is left (for once) to the reader's imagination.

PRIEST: Now that you have reached the fatal moment when the veil of illusion is torn aside only to enable the misguided man to see the cruel tableau of his vices and mistakes, do you not repent, my son, of the manifold errors to which weakness and human frailty have led you?

DYING MAN: Yes, my friend, I repent.

PRIEST: Profit then from this blessed remorse to obtain from Heaven, in the short interval which remains to you, general absolution for your sins, and consider that it is only by the mediation of the very holy sacrament of penitence that you may receive it from the eternal God.

DYING MAN: I understand you no more than you understood me.

PRIEST: What?

DYING MAN: I told you that I had repented.

PRIEST: I heard it.

DYING MAN: Yes, but without understanding it.

PRIEST: What is your interpretation?

DYING MAN: Here is my meaning. I was created by nature with most active tastes, sent into the world solely to surrender myself to them, and to satisfy those desires. As these effects of my creation are only the necessities relative to the first designs of nature, or, if you prefer it, the developments essential to her projects for me, owing to her laws, I repent only that I did not recognize sufficiently all her power, and my sole remorse merely extends to the mediocre use I have made of those faculties (which you would call criminal, I natural) given me by nature for her service. Sometimes I resisted her and that I repent. Blinded by the absurdity of your doctrines, through them I have fought all the violence of the desires communicated to me through a much more divine inspiration, and I repent gathering only flowers when I could have taken a generous harvest of fruit. These are the exact motives for my regrets. Esteem me highly enough not to attribute others to me.

PRIEST: Where are your errors leading you, where are your sophistries taking you! You lend to the thing created all the power of its creator, and you do not see that these unfortunate inclinations which have misguided you are only the effects of this corrupt nature to which you attribute all power.

DYING MAN: It seems to me, friend, that your dialectic is as false as your thought. I wish you would either reason more exactly or leave me to die in peace. What do you mean by creator, and what do you understand by corrupt nature?

PRIEST: The creator is the master of the universe, he who has made all, created all, and who conceives all by a simple effect of his entire power.

DYING MAN: He is a great man, obviously. Now, tell me why such a man who is so powerful has nevertheless made, according to you, a corrupt nature?

PRIEST: What merit would men possess, if God had not left them freedom of choice, and what merit would they enjoy if there were not on this earth the possibility of doing good, and that of avoiding evil?

DYING MAN: And so your God has wished to make everything crooked solely to tempt or to try his creature. Does he not know that creature then, is he in any doubt of the result?

PRIEST: He knows him, doubtless, but once again he wishes to leave him the merit of choosing.

DYING MAN: To what good, once he knows the decision his creature will take, and only holds to it, since you call him all-powerful, to make him choose the good?

PRIEST: Who can understand the immense infinite designs of God for man? Who can understand all that we see?

DYING MAN: He who simplifies things, my friend. Above all, he who does not multiply causes the better to confuse effects. What need is there for a second difficulty when you cannot explain the first? Since it is possible that nature alone has made all that you attribute to your God, why look for a master for her? The cause of that which you cannot understand is perhaps the most simple thing in the world. Improve your physics and you will understand nature better, purify your reasoning, banish your prejudices, and you will no longer need your God.

PRIEST: Unhappy man, I thought you only a Socinian, and I had arms with which to combat you, but I see indeed that you are an atheist. Since your heart is closed to the immensity of the authentic proofs that we receive every day of the existence of the Creator, I have no more to say to you. You cannot give back the light to a blind man.

DYING MAN: My friend, agree with me on one point, that of two men, the one who is the more blind is he who puts a bandage on his eyes, rather than he who tears it off. You build up, invent and multiply causes. I destroy, I simplify. You pile error upon error. I fight all of them. Which of us is the blind one?

PRIEST: You do not believe in God?

DYING MAN: No, and for a very simple reason. It is quite impossible to believe what one does not understand. There must exist immediate connections between understanding and faith. Understanding is the first nourishment of faith. Where understanding does not have some influence, faith is dead, and in such a case those who claim to have it, deceive themselves. I defy you yourself to believe in the God you preach to me – because you do not know how to prove his existence to me, because you are unable to define him to me, and consequently you do not understand him – since you do not understand him, you can no longer give me a single reasonable proof of him, and finally all that is beyond the limit of the human mind is either illusion or uselessness. As your God can only be one or the other of these two things, I would be a fool to believe in him in the first case, and an imbecile in the second. My friend, prove to me the inertia of matter, and then I will grant you your Creator, prove that nature is not self-sufficient, and I shall allow you to suppose a master for her. Until then, expect nothing from me. I give in only to evidence, which I receive only through my senses. Where they stop, my faith remains powerless. I believe in the sun because I see it. I conceive it as the centre of reunion of all the inflammable matter of nature, its periodic march pleases me without astonishing me. It is an operation of physics, as simple perhaps as those of electricity, but which we are not permitted to understand. What need have I to go any further? Even when you will have built up your God above that, am I any more advanced, shall I not need as much effort to understand the workman as to define his work? Therefore you do me no service by the erection of your chimera, you have troubled my mind but you have not enlightened it, and I owe you only hate for it, not gratitude. Your God is a machine, made by you to serve your passions, and fashioned according to their whim, but as it restricts mine, except the fact that I have overthrown it, and do not, at the very moment when my feeble soul has need of calm and philosophy, come frightening it with your sophistries, which would scare without convincing, and irritate without improving. This soul is my friend, what it has pleased nature it might be, the result, that is to say, of the organs she has been pleased to form in me by virtue of her designs and needs. Since she has an equal need of vices and virtues, when it has pleased her to lead me to the former she has done so, when the latter, she has inspired me with desires for them, and I have followed suit just the same. Look no further than her laws for the sole cause of human inconsequence, and do not seek for any other principles in her laws than her wishes and her needs.

PRIEST: Therefore everything in the world is necessary.

DYING MAN: Certainly.

PRIEST: But if everything is necessary, then everything is regulated.

DYING MAN: Who has said the contrary?

PRIEST: Then who can regulate everything as it is, except an all-wise, all-powerful hand?

DYING MAN: Is it not necessary for powder to flare up if you set a light to it?

PRIEST: Yes.

DYING MAN: And what wisdom do you find in that?

PRIEST: None.

DYING MAN: It is possible then that things may be necessary without wisdom, and possible therefore that everything may stem from a first cause which has within it neither reason nor wisdom.

PRIEST: What are you trying to prove?

DYING MAN: To prove to you that all can be as it is, and as you see it, without any wise or reasonable cause to guide it; that natural effects must have natural causes without any need to imagine anti-natural ones for them, such as your God would be, who, as I have already told you, would himself need explanation without providing any. Since your God, therefore, is good for nothing, he is entirely useless; there is a great likelihood that all which is useless is null, and all which is null is void. So to convince myself that your God is an illusion I need no other reasoning than that furnished by the certainty of uselessness.

PRIEST: On that ground there seems to me little necessity to speak to you of religion.

DYING MAN: Why not? Nothing amuses me like proof of the excess to which men, on that point, have been able to carry fanaticism and imbecility. These kinds of terrors are so fantastic that to me the picture, although horrible, is always interesting. Answer me frankly, and above all banish egoism. If I were weak enough to let myself be ensnared by your ridiculous arguments on the fabulous existence of the being who makes religion necessary, in what form would you advise me to offer him my worship? Would you have me adopt the reveries of Confucius rather than the absurdities of Brama, should I venerate the great serpent of the negroes, the star of the Peruvians, or Moses' God of Battle? To which of the sects of Muhammad would you have me turn, or what heresy of the Christians would, according to you, be preferable? Be careful how you reply.

PRIEST: Can there be any doubt about it?

DYING MAN: It is therefore egotistical.

PRIEST: No, to advise what I believe in is to love you as much as myself.

DYING MAN: And it is loving both of ourselves too little to listen to such errors.

PRIEST: Oh! Who can blind himself to the miracles of our divine Redemptor?

DYING MAN: He who sees in him only the most ordinary of all charlatans and the most unconvincing of all impostors.

PRIEST: Oh Gods, you hear him and you do not thunder!

DYING MAN: No, my friend, all is calm, because your God – whether it is from impotence or reason or whatever you will in a being whom I only admit for one moment out of condescension to you, or, if you prefer it, in order to lend myself to your pettiness – because your God, I say, if he exists, as you in your foolishness believe, cannot in order to convince me use means as ridiculous as those your Jesus imagines.

PRIEST: And what of the prophecies, miracles, martyrs – are they not all proofs?

DYING MAN: How can you logically expect me to admit as proof all that which must be proved itself? Before a prophecy can be accepted as proof I must first have absolute assurance that it has been made. Being dependent on history for it, it can have no more force for me than all other historical facts, of which three-quarters are highly doubtful. If I add to that the more than probable supposition that they have been handed down to me only by prejudiced historians,

25

I shall, as you see, be more than right to doubt them. Who can assure me, furthermore, that this prophecy has not been made after the event, that it has not been the effect of the combination of that very simple policy which sees a happy reign under a just king – or frost in wintertime. And if that is so, how can you hope that prophecy, being in such need of proof, can itself become a proof? As for your miracles, they impress me no more. All the tricksters have performed them, and all the blockheads have believed them. To persuade me of the truth of a miracle, I must be quite sure that the event which you so call a miracle was in fact absolutely contrary to the laws of nature, for only something outside them can pass for a miracle; who knows enough of nature to dare to say that at this point precisely she stops, and at this moment precisely she is transgressed? Only two things are needed to give colour to an alleged miracle, a clown and a few feeble men. Well, look no further for the origin of yours, all the new sectarians have them, and, what is strangest, all have found half-wits to believe them. Your Jesus has done nothing more remarkable than Apollonius of Thiana, yet no one pretends to take him for a god. As for your martyrs, they are undoubtedly the feeblest of all your arguments. It needs only fanaticism and resistance to create them; let the other side offer me as much as yours, I should never be sufficiently persuaded to believe one better than the other, but most inclined, on the other hand, to suppose them both pitiful. Oh, my friend, if it were true that the God you preach existed, would he need miracles, martyrs, and prophecies to establish his dominion? If, as you say, the heart of man were his workmanship, would not that be the very sanctuary he would choose for his law? This equal law, since it originates from a just God, would find itself irresistibly engraved in everyone, and from one end of the universe to the other all men, alike in the possession of this sensitive and delicate organ, would be equally alike in the homage they would render the God from whom they hold it. All men would have only one way of loving him, one way of worshipping or serving him, and it would be as impossible for them to ignore this God as to resist the secret attraction of his worship. But what do I see instead in the world – as many gods as countries, as many varieties of service to them as there are different heads or different types of imaginations. Yet, according to you, this multiplicity of opinions amongst which it is physically impossible for me to choose is the work of a just God. Away, preacher, you despoil your God in presenting him to me in that fashion. Leave me to deny him utterly, for if he exists, I offend him less by my disbelief than you by your blasphemies. Come back to the path of reason, preacher, your Jesus is no more worthy than Muhammad, Muhammad no more than Moses, and all three no more than Confucius, who in fact pronounced some good principles while the other three spoke nonsense. But generally, all these people are nothing but impostors, whom the philosopher mocks, the rabble believe, and justice should have caused to hang.

PRIEST: Alas, she did, only too well for one of the four.

DYING MAN: The most deserving of them all. He was seditious, turbulent, slanderous, deceptive, libertine, vulgar actor and dangerous rogue; he possessed the knack of imposing on the people, and therefore became fit for punishment in a kingdom of that state in which Jerusalem was then found. It was very wise to get rid of him, and this is perhaps the only case where my otherwise gentle and tolerant maxims can permit the severity of Themis; I pardon all errors except those which may become dangerous for the government under which we live. Kings and their majesties are the only things which impress me, which I respect – and he who does not love his king and country is not fit to live.

PRIEST: But look, you admit the existence of something after this life; it is impossible that in your mind you have not frequently amused yourself by trying to pierce the thick shadows of the fate which awaits us. What system then can be more satisfactory than one that allots a multitude of punishments for the evildoer and an infinity of blessings for the righteous?

DYING MAN: What, my friend? The idea of oblivion has never frightened me, and it holds only consolation and simplicity for me. All other systems are the product of pride, this alone of reason. Besides, oblivion is neither terrible nor absolute. Do I not see daily examples of the everlasting generation and regeneration of nature? Nothing perishes, my friend, nothing in this world is destroyed. A man today, worms tomorrow, a fly the day after – is this not everlasting life? And why should I be rewarded for virtues which I do not merit, or punished for crimes for which I was never responsible? Can you reconcile the benevolence of your alleged God with such a system? Could he have wanted to create me just for the pleasure of punishing me, and that only because of a choice of which he does not allow me to be master?

PRIEST: But you are.

DYING MAN: Yes, according to your presumptions. But reason destroys them, and the theory of the Freedom of Man was invented only in order to develop that of grace which is so favourable to your dreams. Where in all the world is the man who, seeing the scaffold beside the crime, would still commit it if he were free not to? We are drawn along by an irresistible force, and not for one moment do the masters of that power choose any path for us but that towards which we are inclined. There is not a single virtue which is not necessary to nature, and conversely not a single crime which is not necessary. It is in the perfect balance maintained between one and the other that nature's whole knowledge resides. But can we be blamed for the side on which she casts us? No more than the wasp can be blamed who plunges his sting into your flesh.

PRIEST: And so the greatest of all crimes should inspire no fear in us.

DYING MAN: I did not say so. It is enough for the law to condemn it and the sword of justice punish it to fill us with fear or aversion, but as soon as it is unfortunately committed we must know how to make up our minds and not give way to barren remorse, the effect of which is in vain, since it has not deterred us from committing the crime, and empty since it does not make it good. It is therefore absurd to give way to it, and even more absurd to fear punishment in the other world if we have been lucky enough to escape it in this. God forbid that I intend to encourage crime, it must be avoided wherever possible, but we must learn to abstain from it by reason and not by false fears which come to nothing, and the effects of which are so soon destroyed in any soul with but a little firmness. Reason, yes, my friend, reason alone should warn us that doing harm to our fellows can never make us happy, and our heart should tell us that to contribute to their happiness is the greatest happiness for us that nature allows us on this earth. All human morality is enclosed in this one saying – *Make others as happy as you wish to be yourself* – and never do them more harm than you would be willing to suffer yourself. There, my friend, those are the only principles we need to observe, and there is no call for religion or God to admit and appreciate them. A good heart is all that we need.

But I feel I am getting weaker, preacher. Leave your prejudices, be a man, be human, without fear and without hope. Leave your gods and your religions. All that is of no use except to put weapons into men's hands; the name alone of all those horrors has caused more blood to be shed in the world than all other wars and disasters put together. Renounce the idea of another world – there is none. Do not renounce the pleasure of enjoying and causing happiness in this world. That is the only chance that nature offers you of doubling or extending your existence.

My friend, sensual pleasure was always the dearest of my possessions. I have worshipped it all my life and I wish to embrace it in my end. That end is near. Six women, more lovely than the day, are waiting in this next room; I was reserving them for this moment. Take your share, and try by my example to forget on their breasts all the vain sophistries of superstition, all the ridiculous errors of hypocrisy.

### Note

The dying man rang the bell, and the women entered: in their arms the preacher became a man corrupted by nature because he had not known how to explain what corrupt nature was.

# Les Cent Vingt Journées de Sodome

Is the *Dialogue* disgusting? Ludicrous? Or merely boring? Sade's next writing, after the *Dialogue*, has been dismissed as such, while it has also been seen as his master work. If his later long novels, *La Nouvelle Justine* and *Juliette*, could be regarded at one dismissive level as chapters in the history of obscene fiction, *Les Cent Vingt Journées de Sodome* (The Hundred and Twenty Days of Sodom) is unique.

Sade began work on it while still in prison at the fortress of Vincennes, probably in about 1782 and soon afterwards. He was more than bitter about the injustice of his detention without trial. His health had suffered because he was allowed no exercise, he hated the food and complained about his eyes, which gave him so much pain that his one distraction, writing, was difficult. He had waited three years before being allowed a visit from his wife, but then the visits were stopped following his alleged bad behaviour. His books were taken away. Deprived of everything, he had to write constantly to his wife for sheets, linen, eye-ribbons, sweet biscuits, eau-de-Cologne, night-lights, notebooks.

If his physical life was empty, his head was full of ideas. He now began to write the blackest of his books; blackest because no ray of light, no memory of what might have been happy or 'good' ever gleams through it. Sade conceived and wrote it (part of it, at least) as though the 'normal' world did not exist, and he may well have thought that even if it did, he might never see it again.

The totality of evil portrayed in *Les Cent Vingt Journées* far outstripped the intensity of his own enraged conviction that he was being treated as a non-human creature. Repentance did not preoccupy him for a moment: he knew little beyond rage and a desire for revenge, he was desperate to show that even if his person were confined, in fact *because* he had no liberty, his imagination was totally free, freer than anyone might have thought possible. He took the conscious decision that he would evoke all the potential evil that lay not so much within his own mind as in the mind of man. If society had thought that beating a widow in Paris and feeding aphrodisiacs to girls in Marseille were wicked and punishable, he decided that he would make real all the wickedness that he might have committed but did not. Did his book make him a criminal? The society around him had shown him examples enough of cruelty and perversity, but that was not enough. He wanted, unconsciously, to look into the future, when scientists such as Krafft-Ebbing would attempt to classify sexual perversions. Sade, whose sexual life was now reduced to masturbation, attempted to satisfy himself by presenting all possible aspects of deviant behaviour: 'One cannot imagine to what degree men vary [the passions] when their imagination catches fire,' he wrote. If men were different 'in all their other manias and in all their other tastes', they were even more so where the passions were concerned. He was convinced he was undertaking a valuable task: '. . . he who could establish and detail these deviations would perhaps accomplish one of the finest pieces of work on human customs ever to be seen, and perhaps one of the most interesting'.

Interesting indeed it was, and is. As for the finest, the work earns admiration in the original sense of wonderment. Sade, who was in his early forties, sat alone in his prison cell and worked out the plan of his book with the precision of a mathematician and a careful regard for the characters and the setting. He presumably wished to entertain and instruct his potential readers. He warned them that this would be 'the most impure story ever told', but he maintained that the 'diversity' of the passions described was 'authentic'. Although convinced that he was breaking new ground, he was still ready to use the literary devices of the past, especially when he decided to adopt the story-within-a-story method, as Boccaccio and Marguerite of Navarre had done several centuries earlier, to amuse his 'libertines' during their four months of orgies.

Four friends with vast financial resources, all the time in the world and a total devotion to vice form a kind of sexual consortium. The wives of three of them are involved, plus the daughter of the fourth (who was a bishop), and everyone is interrelated. Four middle-aged women, experienced in prostitution, procuring, perversion and crime, are the latter-day Scheherezade figures and recount anecdotes and longer stories, as well as partaking in the orgies. Other dramatis personae are four elderly women described as duennas, all ugly, deformed or suffering from disgusting diseases. There are eight girls and boys aged between twelve and fifteen, and some lusty young men described as 'the eight fuckers'. Only one of their characteristics is important: the exact size of their penis. The company is dependent on a domestic staff of three cooks and three scullery-maids, for orgiasts need nourishment.

Sade set his book precisely in time – shortly before the death of Louis XIV (in 1715) and equally so in space, taking good care to situate it outside France, in the Château de Silling, deep in the Black Forest and cut off from the real world in all ways. The orgies and the story-telling last from November to February and the company is not to be disturbed: the bridge leading to the château is cut and the doors are sealed.

The sexual activity described in *Les Cent Vingt Journées* is far from sanitized. Rather, it is inextricably mingled with blasphemy (the privies are housed in the chapel), coprophilia and the delights offered by unwashed bodies. Few books written before the twentieth century (the work of Jean Genet comes to mind) have been more preoccupied with extremes of group sex or deviant behaviour, for Sade, bitterly aware of his isolation from society, tried to compensate through portraying an imagined alienation infinitely more extreme than his own.

He also tried to classify the 'passions' he intended to describe into four groups, covering four months of story-telling. These passions were to follow a progression: they would be simple, complex, criminal and finally murderous. If the word 'love' is mentioned occasionally, it is no more than lust, while the ideas that permeate all Sade's major work are never far in the background. Many of them are not original, even if they are intense. He had been deeply impressed by La Mettrie, especially by his book *L'Homme Machine* (1748) and also by Baron d'Holbach, author of *Le Système de la Nature* (1770). Both writers advocated atheistic materialism and Sade the extremist took their beliefs to the furthest lengths he could imagine.

On the Fourth Day of the projected one hundred and twenty Sade's story-teller la Duclos entertains the company with anecdotes about a voyeur and his counterpart, an exhibitionist. She has already described her own early experiences in the high-class house of assignation directed by Madame Guérin.

It should be pointed out that during Sade's lifetime incest and sodomy were punishable by death, but the sentence was rarely carried out. The deaths of children, however, incurred no legal penalty.

## THE FOURTH DAY

Each of the friends* was very keen to distinguish, at every moment of the day, those among the young people, girls and boys, who were destined to grant them their virginity. They decided therefore that in addition to their various forms of dress they must wear a ribbon in their hair indicating to whom they belonged. As a result the duke adopted pink and green, and everyone who wore a pink ribbon in front would belong to him by the cunt, while everyone who wore a green one at the back would belong to him by the arse. From that time Fanny, Zelmire, Sophie and Augustine placed a pink bow at one side of their coiffures and Rosette, Hébé, Michette, Giton and Zéphyr placed a green one at the back of their heads as proof of the rights the duke exercised over their bottoms.

Curval chose a black ribbon for the front and a yellow one for the back, so that in future Michette, Hébé, Colombe and Rosette always wore a black bow in front, while Sophie, Zelmire, Augustine, Zélamit and Adonis placed a yellow one in their chignons.

Durcet distinguished Hyacinthe alone with a lilac ribbon behind and the bishop, who was entitled to only five sodomite deflowerings, ordered Cupidon, Narcisse, Céladon, Colombe and Fanny to wear a violet one at the back.

Whatever clothes were worn these ribbons were never to be changed, and one glance at any of these young people wearing a certain colour in front and another at the back sufficed to show at once who possessed rights over their cunts and who possessed them over their bottoms.

Curval, who had spent the night with Constance, complained about her bitterly in the morning. The reason for these complaints was not clear; it needs so little to displease a

* The Duc de Blangis, Curval, Durcet and an anonymous bishop.

libertine. In any case he was going to have her punished the following Saturday, when this beautiful creature announced that she was pregnant. Curval, the only man, apart from her husband, who could have been suspected as responsible, had known her carnally only since the beginning of the party, that is four days earlier. This news entertained our libertines greatly through the secret pleasures they could clearly see it would bring them. The duke could not get over it. However, the event earned Constance exemption from the penalty she would otherwise have had to undergo for having displeased Curval. They wanted to let the pear ripen, a pregnant woman entertained them and the plans they made for the later developments diverted their perfidious imagination in an even more lewd manner. Constance was excused from waiting at table, from punishments and from a few other minor duties that her state did not render more pleasurable to watch, but she was still obliged to lie on the sofa and to share until further orders the couch of whoever decided to choose her.

That morning it was Durcet who carried out the exercises in pollution and since his prick was remarkably small he caused more difficulties for the young students. However, they worked hard, but the little financier who had played the part of a woman all night could not carry through that of a man. He was impervious, intractable, and the art of those eight delightful students, directed by the most skilful mistress, could not even succeed in making him raise his nose. He emerged from the exercise in total triumph, and since impotence always produces to a small extent the kind of mood described in libertine language as 'teasing', his inspections were astonishingly severe. Rosette among the girls and Zélamir among the boys were the victims: one was not in the state that had been ordered – this enigma will be explained*

* They had disobeyed orders and disposed of their excrement.

– and the other had unfortunately disposed of what he had been told to keep.

In the public places there appeared only la Duclos, Marie, Aline and Fanny, two second-class fuckers and Giton. Curval, who was very randy that day, became inflamed by Duclos. Dinner, during which he made highly libertine remarks, did not calm him down in any way and the coffee, offered by Colombe, Sophie, Zéphyr and his dear friend Adonis, finally set fire to his brain. He seized hold of this boy, threw him down on a sofa and with a curse placed his huge member between his thighs at the back. Since this enormous tool extended more than six inches on the other side, he ordered the boy to masturbate vigorously the part which showed, and he himself began to masturbate the boy above the small piece of flesh by which he held him down. During this time he presented to the assembly a bottom as broad as it was dirty and its orifice tempted the duke. Seeing this arse available to him, he aimed his sinewy instrument while continuing to suck Zéphyr's mouth, an operation he had undertaken before he had had the idea of carrying out what he was now doing.

Curval, who had not been expecting such an onslaught, blasphemed with joy. He quivered in excitement, opened his legs wide and prepared himself. At that moment the youthful sperm of the charming boy he was masturbating dripped down on to the enormous tip of his frenzied instrument. This warm sperm which drenched him, the repeated shuddering of the duke who was beginning to discharge also, everything led him on, everything brought on his climax and floods of foaming sperm flooded Durcet's arse. This latter had posted himself there close by so, as he said, nothing was wasted. His plump white buttocks were softly immersed in an enchanting liquor which he would much have preferred in his entrails.

Meanwhile the bishop was not idle; he sucked alternately the divine arseholes of Colombe and Sophie. However, exhausted no doubt by various nocturnal exercises, he gave no sign of life and like all libertines rendered unjust by caprice and distaste he blamed harshly those two delightful children for the well-deserved weaknesses of his feeble nature.

Everyone dozed for a few minutes and since the hour for story-telling had come they now listened to the amiable Duclos who took up her story again in the following terms:

'There had been a few changes in Madame Guérin's house,' said our heroine.* 'Two very pretty girls had just found some dupes who were ready to keep them, and they deceived them as all women do. In order to make good this loss our dear mother had cast her eyes on the daughter of an innkeeper in the rue Saint Denis. She was thirteen years old and one of the prettiest creatures it was possible to see. But the young person, as well behaved as she was pious, resisted every seduction. Then la Guérin, having found a very skilful method to attract her to the house one day, immediately placed her in the hands of a strange person whose mania I shall describe to you. He was an ecclesiastic of fifty-five or fifty-six, but, fresh and vigorous, he could have been taken for less than forty. Nobody in the world had a more remarkable talent than this man for enticing young girls into vice, and since it was the most sublime of his arts, he made it also into his one and only pleasure. His entire delight consisted of rooting out the prejudices of childhood, causing virtue to be scorned and decking out vice in the most attractive colours. Nothing in this was neglected: seductive pictures, flattering promises, delightful examples, everything was brought into play, everything was skilfully handled, everything artistically geared to the age of the child and her type of intelligence, and he never failed. In a mere two hours of conversation he

---

* She is referring to an earlier description of this establishment.

was certain to turn the best-behaved and the most reasonable little girl into a trollop. During the thirty years in which he had exercised this profession in Paris he had admitted to Madame Guérin, one of his best friends, that he had a catalogue of more than ten thousand young girls whom he had seduced and cast into the libertine life. He carried out the same services for more than fifteen procuresses, and when he was not employed he carried out research on his own account, corrupted everything he found and sent it to his suppliers. For what is most extraordinary, and the reason why I am describing to you the life story of this unusual personage, is that he never enjoyed the fruit of his labours. He would shut himself in with the child, but despite all the resilience supplied by his mind and his eloquence, he would emerge deeply aroused. People were totally convinced that the operation worked on his senses, but it was impossible to know either where or how he satisfied them. Even when he was closely examined, all that could be seen about him at the end of his talk was a remarkably fiery look and a few movements of his hand over the front of his breeches which indicated a distinct erection produced by the diabolical work he was carrying out, but never anything else.

'He arrived, he was shut in with the innkeeper's young daughter, I observed him. The tête-à-tête was lengthy, the seducer put into it an astonishing degree of pathos, the child cried, became animated, appeared to enter into a kind of enthusiasm. This was the moment when the man's eyes shone most brightly and when we noticed his gestures over the front of his breeches. Shortly afterwards he stood up, the child held out her arms as though to embrace him, he kissed her like a father and showed no kind of lewd attitude. He left, and three hours later the girl arrived at Madame Guérin's with her things.'

'And what about the man?' asked the duke.

'He had vanished immediately after his lesson,' replied Duclos.

'Without returning to see the result of his work?'

'No, monseigneur, he was sure of success. Not a single lesson had ever failed.'

'So there is a very extraordinary character,' said Curval. 'What do you think of him, monsieur le duc?'

'I think', replied the latter, 'that he was merely aroused by this seduction and that he discharged into his breeches.'

'No,' said the bishop, 'you haven't understood. This was only a preparation for his debaucheries and I wager that after this he was going on to commit some more serious ones.'

'More serious ones?' said Durcet. 'And what more delightful pleasure could he have derived than that of enjoying his own handiwork, since he was in control of it?'

'Well', said the duke, 'I wager I've found the answer. This as you say was merely a preparation, he aroused his feelings by corrupting young girls, and went on to sodomize boys . . . he was a bugger, I'll wager.'

They asked Duclos if she had any proof of this supposition, and if the man didn't also seduce young boys. Our storyteller replied that she had no proof of this, and despite the duke's very convincing assertion, everyone remained none the less in doubt about the nature of this strange preacher. It was generally agreed that his mania was truly delightful, but that he needed either to consummate the act or do something worse afterwards. Then Duclos took up the thread of her story again in the following manner:

'The day after our young novice, who was called Henriette, had come to the house, there arrived an eccentric lecher who brought the girl and myself together for the same task. This new libertine enjoyed no other pleasure beyond observing through a hole in the wall all the somewhat unusual delights which were being experienced in a nearby room. He liked to spy on them and found thus in the pleasures of others a divine form of encouragement to his own lewdness. He was placed in the room to which I have already referred and into which I went very often, as my colleagues did, to spy for my own pleasure on the passions of the libertines. I was chosen to amuse him while he carried out his examinations, and the young Henriette went into the other room with the arsehole-sucker of whom I spoke to you yesterday. The highly voluptuous passion of this lecher was the show that we wished to present to my observer, and in order to arouse him more deeply, rendering the scene more heated and more pleasant to watch, he was told in advance that the girl who had been allotted to him was a novice and that it was with him that she was fulfilling her first assignment. He was easily convinced of this through the modest and childlike manner of the little tavern-keeper's daughter. As a result he was as highly inflamed and lecherous as it was possible to be in his lewd performance, and he had no idea they were being observed. As for my man, who had his eye glued to the hole, with one hand on my bottom and the other on his prick which he was gradually stroking, he seemed to be matching his ecstasy to what he was observing. "Ah, what a sight!" he would say from time to time. "What a fine bottom that little girl has and how well that bugger is kissing it." In the end, after Henriette's lover had discharged, mine took me in his arms, and after having kissed me for a moment he turned me round, fondled, kissed and licked my bottom in obscene fashion and drenched my buttocks with the proofs of his virility.'

'While masturbating himself?' asked the duke.

'Yes, monseigneur,' replied la Duclos, 'while rubbing a prick, which I assure you, was so incredibly small that it is not worth a detailed description.'

'The personage who appeared afterwards', Duclos continued, 'might not have deserved to appear on my list if he had not seemed to me worthy of being pointed out through one attitude, rather strange as I see it, which formed part of his pleasures, fairly simple ones in fact. It will make you see to what extent libertinage degrades in a man all feelings of modesty, virtue and humility. This man did not wish to see, he wished to be seen. And knowing that there were men whose dream was to watch the pleasures of others, he begged la Guérin to hide a man with those tastes, who would provide him with the spectacle of his pleasures. La Guérin alerted the man whom I had entertained a few days earlier in front of the hole in the wall, without telling him that the man whom he was going to see knew very well that he would be seen – which would have disturbed his pleasure. She made him believe that in comfort he was going to watch the show about to be offered to him.

'The viewer was shut into the room with the hole in the wall, with my sister, and I went through with the other man. He was a young man of twenty-eight, handsome and fresh. After being told about the location of the hole he took up his position opposite to it in a casual manner and arranged for me to stand beside him. I masturbated him. As soon as he began to have an erection he stood up, displayed his prick to the observer, turned round, showed his arse, pulled up my skirts, showed mine, knelt down in front of it, rubbed my anus with the tip of his nose, exhibited everything with delight and precision and discharged while masturbating himself, at the same time holding me, with my skirts up, in front of the hole. In this way the man standing on the other side of it saw at this decisive moment both my bottom and my lover's raging prick. If this latter man experienced pleasure, God knows what the other man felt; my sister said he was transported with delight, he admitted that he had never felt so much happiness, and after that his buttocks were flooded just as much as mine had been.'

'If the young man had a fine prick and a fine bottom,' said Durcet, 'there must have been good reason for a splendid discharge.'

'It must have been delicious then,' said Duclos, 'for his prick was very long, fairly solid, and his bottom was as soft, as chubby, as prettily formed, as that of love itself.'

'Did you separate his buttocks?' asked the bishop. 'Did you display the hole to the observer?'

'Yes, monseigneur,' said Duclos, 'he showed mine, I offered his, he presented it in the most lewd manner in the world.'

'I've seen a dozen scenes like that in my life,' said Durcet, 'which have cost me a lot of sperm. There are few things more delightful to do. I speak of both aspects, for it's as enjoyable to watch as it is to want to be watched.'

'A person with more or less the same tastes', Duclos went on, 'took me to the Tuileries gardens a few months later. He wanted me to procure men for him and masturbate them right under his nose, in the middle of a pile of chairs in which he had concealed himself. And after I had aroused seven or eight for him in this way he sat down on a bench in one of the most frequented of the alleyways, pulled my skirts up at the back, revealed my bottom to the passers-by, brought out his prick and ordered me to frig it in front of all of them, and although it was dark this caused such a scandal that when he shamelessly released his sperm there were more than ten people around us. We were obliged to run away in order to avoid being disgraced.

'When I told our story to la Guérin she laughed and told me that she had once known a man in Lyon (where boys act as panders) whose mania was at least just as strange. He disguised himself as a public go-between, took people himself to two girls whom he paid and kept for that reason, then hid in a corner to watch his plan in action. This latter, directed by the girl whom he had been bribing for this purpose, did not fail to show him the prick and bottom of the libertine she was clasping, the only pleasure to the taste of our false go-between, and the one capable of making him lose his sperm.'

Since Duclos had finished her story early that evening the friends spent the rest of the time, before supper was served, in a few choice lecheries. And since they had been aroused by shameless behaviour, they did not go into the private rooms and all entertained themselves in front of each other. The duke had la Duclos completely undressed, made her bend down, leaning against the back of a chair and ordered la Desgranges to masturbate him over her friend's buttocks, so that the tip of his prick brushed against Duclos's arsehole with every movement. A few other episodes followed which the order of this material does not yet allow us to reveal: however, the story-teller's arsehole was entirely drenched, the duke was very well served and taken care of. He discharged with cries, which proved to what point he was aroused. Curval had himself fucked, the bishop and Durcet did very strange things with both sexes, then supper was served.

After supper there was dancing, the sixteen young people, four fuckers and the four wives were able to perform three quadrilles, but all the participants in this ball were naked and our libertines, as they lay nonchalantly on the sofas, were delightfully entertained by all the different beauties offered to them in turn by the various attitudes that the dancing led the performers to assume. The libertines had near to them the story-tellers, who caressed them more or less quickly depending on the degree of enjoyment experienced by the men but, exhausted by the pleasures of the day, no one discharged, and each of them went to bed in order to find the necessary strength with which to abandon themselves the next day to new expressions of infamy.

Sade had planned many 'new expressions of infamy' which were to grow deeper and more horrifying as his story-tellers proceeded, but in the end he wrote out in detail only the first thirty days of the hundred and twenty. La Duclos completes her duties at the end of November. The author then acted as his own editor and made a list of his 'mistakes': he had said too much, he thought, about the activities in the chapel (i.e. the privies) and too much about sodomy, active and passive. The remaining months of orgies and stories are recounted only in note form. During December Madame Champville, who was faithfully devoted to Sappho, narrates the 'complex' passions. January sees Madame Martaine, who had spent her life in sodomite debauchery (a physical deformity prevented any other form of sex life), describing the 'criminal' passions, while Madame Desgranges, who personifies vice and lust, completes the winter with the 'murderous' passions. They are so murderous, and have such an effect on the listeners, that the former friends begin to kill each other by various nauseating methods. In the end only sixteen out of the original forty-six libertines and their staff survive and return to Paris. The four ringleaders avoid murder, but their wives are sacrificed. The story-tellers are allowed to go on living, and if the scullery-maids are dispatched, the three cooks, owing to their 'considerable talents', survive.

There were many possible reasons why Sade did not complete his vast book – eye-strain may have been one of them. The poet Guillaume Apollinaire, who learnt enough from Sade to write pornographic novels himself, gives one ironic, flippant explanation of why only a quarter or so of the projected work was finished: 'He must have been short of paper'.

# Lettre XXIII

## To Madame de Sade

The year 1784 introduced a new chapter in Sade's life, for without warning he was removed from Vincennes and transferred to the Bastille prison in the heart of Paris. The transfer took place on 29th February. The prisoner, who was not allowed to take anything with him, now found himself in a small octagonal room on the second floor of one of the towers. He had complained enough while in Vincennes but now, writing to his wife a week or so after the move, he complained about everything. He was ready to make his bed, as he had been told to do, but he was not good at sweeping the floor. Ironically, he hoped he might learn the skill by watching the man whose duty it might have been. To his chagrin, he was now much worse off than he had been in Vincennes. He wrote to Madame de Sade more in sorrow than in anger.

*(Bastille, 8th March 1784)*

Thirty-four months after an express refusal of a transfer to a fortress at the very door of my estates where every liberty was offered me, after a petition to end my days in peace where I was, wicked though I might be, all the time it pleased your mother to sacrifice me to her revenge, thirty-four months, I repeat, after this event, to see myself now

47

forcibly removed unexpectedly and without warning, with all this mystery, all this comic incognito, all this enthusiasm, all this zeal scarcely pardonable in the excitement of the most important affair and after twelve years of misfortunes, as banal as it is ridiculous! And to see myself transferred to a prison in which I am worse off and a thousand times more constricted than in the wretched place where I was before! Such actions, Madame, with whatever odious lies you attempt to palliate their atrocious blackness, such actions, you must confess, deserve the culmination of all the hatred I have sworn against your infamous family. And I think that you would be the first to despise me if the acts of vengeance did not one day rival all the ferocious repetitions of theirs. But keep calm and rest assured that neither you nor the public will have anything to reproach me with on that score. But I shall have neither the virtue nor the perseverance to invent or search out in a *cold rage* whatever can render more bitter the venom which I ought to use. Everything will rise up from within me; I shall give my heart a chance, allow it free play in the sure knowledge that the serpents it will produce will be at least as poisonous as those which are hurled against me.

But let us pass on to the details. It is deeds not words that are required in this case, and while one's arms are tied, one must keep silent. These are the lessons in treachery that they have taught me; I shall profit by them, yes, profit, and one day I shall be as deceitful as you.

For twenty years, Madame, you have known that it is absolutely impossible for me to tolerate a room with a stove, and yet it is (thanks to the attentions of those who have concerned themselves with my transference) in a room of that kind that I am now shut up. I have been so incommoded these days that I have stopped lighting fires, and that whatever the weather, I shall continue not to light any. Luckily summer is here; but if I am to be here next winter, I implore you to see that I have a room with a fireplace.

You know that exercise is more important to me than food. And yet here I am in a room half the size of the one I had before. I haven't room to swing a cat and I can leave it only rarely to go into a narrow yard where you can breathe only guardroom and cookhouse air and into which I am marched at the point of the bayonet as if I had attempted to dethrone Louis XVI! Oh, how they make one despise great things when they endow little things with such importance!

The turns of dizziness to which I am subject, the frequent attacks of nose-bleedings which I suffer when I lie down without a very high support for my head, have forced me, as you know, to have a very large pillow. When I wanted to bring away the wretched pillow, you would think I was trying to steal the list of conspirators against the State; they snatched it out of my hands, protesting that acts of such consequence had never been tolerated. And in point of fact I saw that some secret decree of the government required a prisoner to sleep with his head low, for when, as a substitute for this pillow of which they deprived me I humbly requested four miserable planks of wood, they took me for a madman. A host of officials descended on me and having verified that I was very badly bedded, gave the judgement that it was not the custom for one to be otherwise. I protest to you in truth that these things must be seen to be believed, and that if they told us that they happened in China, our soft-hearted and sympathetic French would immediately cry out: 'Oh, the savages!'

Furthermore they claim that I must make my bed and sweep out my room; the first, I don't mind, because they did it very badly and it amuses me to do it. But as for that second, unfortunately I cannot manage it at all; my parents must be to blame for not having included that particular skill in my education. The fact is there were many things they did not foresee . . . many things. If they had, there would have been no tavern wench who could have rivalled me.

Meanwhile I beg you to persuade the authorities to give me some lessons. Let the man who looks after me sweep it out but once a week for four or five years; I shall *study* him closely and you will see that afterwards I shall manage as well as he.

For seven years I have enjoyed the use of knives and scissors at Vincennes without causing any inconvenience. I haven't improved the last seven years, of that I am well aware, but neither have I deteriorated. Could you not make that point so as to persuade them to allow me the complete use of those two objects?

I am naked, thank God, and soon I shall be as I was when I emerged from my mother's womb: I was not allowed to bring anything with me; a shirt, a night-cap caused the guard to swear and Rougemont to shout himself hoarse. So I have abandoned everything, and I beg you to bring with you without fail on your first visit – two shirts, two handkerchiefs, six towels, three pairs of list-shoes, four pairs of cotton stockings, two cotton night-caps, two headbands, a black taffeta cap, two muslin cravats, a dressing-gown, four small pieces of cloth five square inches which I need for bathing my eyes, and some of the books that are on my previous list. All this on condition that I receive my boxes and other possessions from Vincennes inside a fortnight, for, if I had to go any longer without receiving them, all those items would have to be duplicated or triplicated, because of the time you anticipated that I should still be without my luggage.

Add to those things, I beg you, the following objects which bear no relation to the trunks, that is to say I am in constant need of them whether I receive my clothes soon or late. (Pressing items: my tail-cushion which I left at Vincennes, my fur-lined slippers, my two mattresses and my pillow.)

Half a dozen pots of preserves; half a dozen pounds of candles; some packets of small ones of fifteen to the packet; a pint of eau-de-Cologne of better quality than the last which was no use at all; a pint of rose-water for my eyes, into which you have first put one sixth part of brandy, that is to say five parts of rose-water to one of brandy to the pint; and the rest of the books which I long ago requested together with what was left of the new comedies to fill the catalogue I sent.

Let me have the objects requested in this letter if that is possible so that I may at least say that, for once, you have been useful for something during my detention, and above all the two mattresses for my bed and my large pillow. I leave the rest to our friend in charge.

If the oculists tell you that sea-water and the powder in question are still necessary for my eye, which is still in the same wretched state, get them to send me these objects left at Vincennes.

Expedite the dispatch of my luggage, I beg you.

Ah well! my very dear, very amiable and above all very ingenuous wife, were you carrying out a pretty deception on me when on each of your visits you promised that it would be you who would come to collect me, that I should come out a free man and see my children! Is it possible to be more basely deceitful and false? And now tell me if you believe that those who authorize you to deceive your husband so foully work for the happiness of your life? . . . My dear wife, if they tell you that, they are deceiving you: tell them that it is I who assure you of it.

Since my return to Vincennes after all the previous horrors which I at any rate have not forgotten, since this return there remained but two dagger thrusts that you and your people could inflict: change my prison and pack my son off to a corps in which I am absolutely opposed to his serving, and without my seeing him. Both these blows you have delivered. I shall not be ungrateful, this I swear on what I hold most sacred in the world.

I send my humble greetings, Madame, and implore you to pay some attention to my letter, my requests and commissions, all the more since part of my new plan of life here is to send you nothing but lists, by which token here is my first and last letter.

*[In the right-hand margin]*

(PS.) I think you would do well to reward the guard officer for services on which I can only congratulate myself and all the more because I am now so cruelly aware of the present difference. I commend him to you.

*(Translated from the French by W.J. Strachan)*

If the prisoner-author had completed the first thirty days of his projected one hundred and twenty, the sudden transfer to the Bastille in 1784 made him doubly aware that his writing had become his life. Without his manuscript, what was left to him? Since he had not been allowed to take his papers or any of his books with him, he saw that his career as a writer was as fragile as his hope of liberty. His manuscript could easily have been lost or confiscated by the authorities. He was lucky: it followed him, with his other possessions, to his cell in the Bastille, presumably because nobody had had time to read it. Sade now seems to have felt that it was more important to make a fair copy of what he had written so far than to continue. He spent just over a month on his self-imposed task, after which this partial manuscript embarked on an adventurous life of its own, described by Apollinaire early in the twentieth century and much quoted since. 'The manuscript is formed of sheets of paper 11 centimetres long stuck together and forming a roll 12 metres 10 in length. It is written on both sides in near-microscopic handwriting.' It was then hidden, and must have been well hidden, otherwise, as will become obvious later, it might have disappeared for ever. 'This manuscript', writes Apollinaire, 'is said to have been found in the room occupied by the Marquis de Sade in the Bastille by Arnoux Saint-Maximin, who gave it to the grandfather of the Marquis de Villeneuve-Trans, in whose family it remained for three generations.'

The last owner of the manuscript had apparently kept it in a phallic-shaped box. At the very end of the nineteenth century a new personage entered the story, Dr Iwan Bloch, a German doctor who wrote under the name of Eugen Dühren. 'Doctor Dühren', Apollinaire continues, 'arranged for it to be sold, through a Paris bookseller, to a German collector at a high price.' Presumably this allowed Bloch-Dühren to publish it, for the first time, in 1904.

As for the prisoner-author, back in 1785, after he had transcribed and concealed the twelve metres of sodomistic narrative, he now embarked on some of the busiest years of his writing life. During 1787 and 1788 he was preoccupied for the first time with conventional story-telling more or less in tune with the taste of the age. He had read most of the popular contemporary authors from Voltaire, Marmontel and Prévost to Crébillon, Restif de la Bretonne and lesser 'libertine' writers. He had a particular admiration for Madame de La Fayette and also for the English novelists Richardson and Fielding. In a letter written to his wife in 1783, after listing what he saw as his 'virtues' and his 'vices', he concludes by saying: ' . . . either kill me or take me as I am, for I shall not change'. In essence he never did, but most of the stories and the long novel he now wrote reveal aspects of this complex man which could hardly have been anticipated by a reading of *Les Cent Vingt Journées de Sodome*.

In fact nobody had read this piece of literary onanism and several more years would pass before anyone could read any of the *Contes, Historiettes et Fabliaux d'un Troubadour Provençal*, or the stories known as *Les Crimes de l'Amour*. The precise dates of their composition and their bibliographical history are not entirely clear, the literary merits of many are dubious, but in certain ways they have great value: they are accessible to the twentieth-century reader, they are never too long and they can hold the attention by a variety of means, varying from ironic humour or crude farce to psychological insight or Gothic horror. One of the best known, *Le Magistrat Mystifié* (The Mystified Magistrate), based partly on his own conviction at Aix, contains no references to the serious charges laid against him and express Sade's revenge through a harshly comic attack on an imaginary president. In another story, *Faxelange*, the author shows how an arranged marriage can lead ambitious parents and the bride herself into trouble, while in *La Comtesse de Sancerre* he may have planned a form of revenge against his mother-in-law, for the countess is in love with her daughter's intended husband and is prepared to commit any crime in order to keep him to herself.

# La Châtelaine de Longeville

## ou La Femme Vengée

In *La Châtelaine de Longeville** (or The Avenged Wife) Sade wished to entertain his readers and at the same time aim ironic laughter at the way the aristocrats lived under the despotic regimes of earlier centuries. Either he sensed that their way of life was about to change or he wrote the story after that change had begun. This farcical tale includes a heartless heroine ready to arrange her rival's murder, and perhaps in a not too serious way she foreshadows Sade's famous and totally depraved Juliette. The Châtelaine of Longeville, more subtle than her clumsy, snobbish husband, is one of the many signs in Sade's work that he considered women to be more intelligent than men.

During the times when seigneurs lived despotically on their estates, during those glorious times when France counted within her boundaries a host of sovereigns, instead of thirty thousand lowly slaves prostrate before a single one, there lived in the midst of his domains the seigneur of Longeville, owner of a fairly large property near Fismes in Champagne. He had a little dark-haired wife, mischievous, very lively, not really pretty but roguish and passionately fond of pleasure:

* Longeville is spelt thus in Sade's *catalogue raisonné* of 1788. In subsequent editions it is spelt Longueville.

the lady châtelaine could have been twenty-five to twenty-six years old and monsieur thirty at the most. They had been married for ten years and both being of an age to seek some slight distractions from the boredom of marriage they attempted to find in the neighbourhood the best ones available. The village or rather the hamlet of Longeville offered few resources; however, a little farm-girl of eighteen, very appetizing and fresh, had discovered the secret of pleasing monseigneur and for two years he had had the best possible arrangement with her. Louison, the name of the beloved turtle-dove, would come every evening to her master's bed by taking a concealed staircase built in one of the towers adjoining the master's apartment and in the morning she would decamp before madame joined her husband, as she usually did, for breakfast.

Madame de Longeville was in no way unaware of her husband's unseemly conduct, but since on her side she was quite pleased to entertain herself also, she said nothing: no one is as submissive as unfaithful wives; it is so important for them to conceal their own actions that they criticize those of others much less than prudes would do. A local miller named Colas, a young rascal of eighteen or twenty, his skin as white as his own flour, and as attractive as the roses which grew in his little garden, came every evening like Louison into a closet near madame's apartment and when everything was quiet in the château he quickly got into the bed. It was impossible to find anything more tranquil than those little ménages; without the demon which interfered in them I am sure they could have been quoted as exemplary throughout the whole of Champagne.

Do not laugh, reader, no, do not laugh in any way at this word exemplary; if virtue is absent, then decent and well-concealed vice can serve as a model: is it not as successful as it is skilful to sin without scandalizing one's fellows and in fact what danger can there be in wrongdoing when it remains unknown? Let us see – you will decide – was this minor misconduct not preferable to the picture offered us by the life-style of today? Do you not prefer the sire of Longeville quietly in the pretty arms of his pretty farm-girl, and his respectable wife in the embrace of a handsome miller whose happiness is unknown to you, to one of our Parisian duchesses publicly changing her *cicisbeo* every month, or giving herself to her valets, while monsieur consumes two hundred thousand écus a year with one of those despicable creatures disguised by luxury, degraded by birth and corrupted by virtue? I say therefore that without the discord whose poisons will soon spread over these four favourites of love, there was nothing more agreeable and better conducted than their charming little arrangement.

But the sire of Longeville, like many unjust husbands, had the cruel wish to be happy and did not want his wife to be so. He imagined as partridges do that nobody could see him because his head was concealed. He discovered his wife's intrigue and found it wrong, as though his own conduct did not fully authorize that which he took upon himself to criticize.

To a jealous mind the distance from discovery to revenge is not long. Monsieur de Longeville decided therefore to say nothing and to get rid of the odd young man who was making horns sprout on his forehead. To be made a cuckold, he said to himself, by a man of my own rank, that's all very well, but by a miller, oh Monsieur Colas, please be good enough to go a-grinding at another mill, it shall not be said that my wife's mill opens wider to accept your seed. And since the hatred of these little ruling despots was always very cruel, since they often abused the right to life and death over their vassals accorded to them by feudal laws, Monsieur de Longeville decided on nothing less than having poor Colas thrown into the moat that surrounded his dwelling.

'Clodomir,' he said one day to his steward, 'you and your boys must rid me of a scurvy peasant who is defiling madame's bed.'

'It shall be done, monsieur,' replied Clodomir. 'We shall slit his throat if you wish and serve him up to you trussed like a sucking-pig.'

'No, my friend,' replied Monsieur de Longeville, 'he need only be placed in a sack containing stones and thrown down like that into the château moat.'

'It shall be done.'

'Yes, but first of all we have to catch him and we haven't got him.'

'We shall get him, monsieur, he'll be very clever if he escapes us. We shall get him, I tell you.'

'He will come this evening at nine o'clock,' said the wronged husband. 'He will come through the garden, arrive directly in the ground-floor rooms, go and hide in the closet near the chapel and remain crouching there until madame, when she thinks I am asleep, will come to get him out and take him to her apartment. We must let him go through all his procedures, be content to lie in wait for him and as soon as he believes he is safe we shall take hold of him and send him to drink in order to cool his ardour.'

Nothing was better organized than this plan and if everyone had been discreet poor Colas was certainly going to be eaten by the fish. But the baron had confided in too many people, he was betrayed. A young kitchen-hand, who loved the châtelaine and perhaps hoped to share her favours with the miller one day, obeying the feeling inspired by his mistress rather than by the jealousy that might have left him delighted by the misfortune of his rival, hastened to disclose everything that was being plotted. He was rewarded by a kiss and two fine golden écus which for him had less value than the kiss.

'Undoubtedly,' said Madame de Longeville, as soon as she was alone with the maid who assisted her in her intrigue, 'monsieur is a very unjust man, he does as he wants, I say nothing, and he finds it wrong that I compensate for all the days of deprivation he causes me. Ah! I shan't tolerate it, my dear, I shan't tolerate it. Listen, Jeannette, are you the kind of girl to help me in the plan that I'm concocting both to save Colas and catch out monseigneur?'

'Certainly, madame has only to give orders, I'll do everything. The good Colas is a decent boy, I've never seen any other boy with such a strong back and such a fresh complexion. Oh yes, madame, oh yes, I'll carry out your orders, what must I do?'

'You must go immediately', said the lady, 'and warn Colas not to appear at the château until I tell him, and ask him on my behalf to lend me the complete set of clothing that he usually wears when he comes here. As soon as you have these clothes, Jeannette, you will go and find Louison, my faithless husband's beloved, and you will tell her that you've come on monsieur's behalf: he enjoins her to put on the clothes that you will be carrying in your apron, she must no longer come by her usual route, but through the garden, the courtyard and the ground-floor rooms, and as soon as she is inside the house she must hide in the closet which is by the chapel* until monsieur comes for her.

'As she will surely question you about these changes, you will say that they are caused by madame's jealousy, for madame has discovered everything and is having her watched along the way she usually takes. If she is frightened you will reassure her, you will give her some gift and you will tell her that on no account must she fail to come this evening, for monsieur has very important things to tell her about what followed the scene of madame's jealousy.'

Jeannette left, carried out the two errands as well as she could and at nine o'clock it was the unfortunate Louison, dressed in Colas's clothes, who was in the closet where the men proposed to take madame's lover by surprise.

'Let us advance,' said Monsieur de Longeville to his men,

* All these places still exist at the Château de Longeville. (Author's note)

who like him had been continually on the look-out, 'let us advance. You've all seen him as I did, my friends, haven't you?'

'Yes, monseigneur. My word, he's a good-looking boy.'

'Open the door quickly, throw some clothes over his head to stop him crying out, push him into the sack and drown him without more ado.'

Everything went according to plan, they stopped the mouth of the unfortunate captive so that her cries could not be heard, she was pushed into the sack which contained some large stones and, through the window of the closet where she had been captured, she was thrown into the middle of the moat.

Once the deed was done everyone dispersed and Monsieur de Longeville went to his apartment, very impatient to receive the damsel who, he thought, would not be long in coming and who, quite unknown to him, was in such a chilly place. Half the night passed and no one appeared. Since there was beautiful moonlight, our anxious lover decided to go himself to his loved one's house to see what had kept her away. He went out and during that time Madame de Longeville, who had missed none of his actions, got into her husband's bed.

Monsieur de Longeville learned at Louison's house that she had gone out as usual and that she was certainly at the château; they told him nothing about the disguise because Louison had not mentioned it to anyone and she had slipped out without being seen.

The master returned and since the candle he had left burning in his room had gone out he went close to his bed to find a tinder-box in order to light it again. As he approached he heard breathing and was certain that his dear one had arrived while he was out looking for her and, not seeing him in his apartment, had impatiently got into bed. He therefore did not hesitate one moment and was soon between the sheets, caressing his wife with loving words and tender expressions which he had been wont to use with his beloved Louison.

'How long you made me wait, my dear one . . . where were you then, my dear Louison . . .'

'Faithless man,' said Madame de Longeville, opening a dark lantern that she had kept hidden, 'so I can no longer doubt your conduct, recognize your wife, and not the slut to whom you have been giving what belongs only to me.'

'Madame,' replied the husband, showing no surprise, 'I think I am master of my actions, when you yourself fail me in such essential matters.'

'Fail you, monsieur, and in what, pray?'

'Do I not know about your intrigue with Colas, one of the most humble peasants on my estate?'

'I, monsieur?' replied the châtelaine in arrogant tones. 'I, lower myself to that extent, you are imagining it! Not one word of what you are saying is true and I challenge you to give me proof of it.'

'It's true, madame, that it would be difficult at the moment, for I have just had the wretch who was dishonouring me thrown into the moat, and you will never see him again.'

'Monsieur,' said the châtelaine, with even more effrontery, 'if you have had that wretched man thrown into the water on suspicions of that sort you are certainly guilty of a great injustice, but if, as you say, he is punished this way only because he came into the château, I am very much afraid you are mistaken, for he never set foot there in his life.'

'In truth, madame, you could make me believe I'm mad.'

'Let us explain matters, monsieur, let us explain. Send Jeannette here yourself to find this peasant of whom you are so wrongly and ridiculously jealous, and we shall see the result.'

The baron agreed, Jeannette left and returned with Colas in good shape. Monsieur de Longeville rubbed his eyes on seeing him, he immediately ordered everyone to go and find out as quickly as possible who, in this case, was the individual he had had cast into the moat. They rushed out, but they brought back only a corpse and it was that of the unfortunate Louison which was displayed to her lover.

'O merciful heaven,' cried the baron, 'an unknown hand is at work in all this, but it is providence that directs it, and I shall not complain about the blows it delivers. Whether it is you or anyone else, madame, who is responsible for this blunder, I renounce any attempt to investigate it. Now that you are rid of the girl who was causing you anxiety, rid me in the same way of the man who has been worrying me, and may Colas disappear from the region. Do you agree, madame?'

'I shall go further, monsieur. I join you in ordering him to do so: may there be peace between us again, may love and esteem recover their rights and may nothing separate them in future.'

Colas departed and did not appear again. Louison was buried and since that time in the whole of Champagne no husband and wife were ever more united than the lord and lady of Longeville.

# Aline et Valcour
## ou Le Roman Philosophique

In the late 1780s Sade was not only writing short stories and novellas, he was working on a long novel, *Aline et Valcour – le roman philosophique*, as he called it, which was published eventually in 1795. He was very proud of this novel, planned as an exchange of seventy-two letters written mainly by or about the hero and heroine of the title, and containing stories subsidiary to the main plot. It is of great interest, biographical, sociological and literary. It reveals Sade as a writer in the heroic style, and also Sade the social critic exposing the horrors of the arranged marriage system, from which he himself had suffered. The element of cruelty, as in the stories forming *Les Crimes de l'Amour*, is almost entirely psychological, not physical.

It was a 'good read' when it was published and still is, for there is no shortage of suspense, especially in the principal related story, *L'Histoire de Sainville et de Léonore*. There is a widening of Sade's vision, a corrective to the nihilism of the earlier *Les Cent Vingt Journées*, and also to *La Nouvelle Justine* and *Juliette*, which had not yet reached their final versions. The iconoclast was now anxious to prove himself a democrat.

In Lettre V Valcour tells Aline the story of his life so far:

I shall say little to you about my birth; you are acquainted

63

with it: I shall tell you only about the errors into which I was led by the illusion of a vain origin about which we pride ourselves almost always with little reason, since this advantage is due only to chance.

Through my mother I was allied to everything that was greatest in the kingdom; through my father I was related to everything that was most distinguished in Languedoc. Born in Paris in the midst of luxury and riches I believed, as soon as I was able to reason, that nature and fortune had combined in order to shower their riches upon me. I believed it, for people had been stupid enough to tell me so, and this absurd prejudice made me haughty, despotic and quick to anger. It seemed that everything should yield to me, that the entire universe should give way before my caprices, that I needed only to formulate them and they would at once be satisfied. I shall recount to you one simple incident from my childhood to convince you of the dangerous principles that others so foolishly allowed to take root within me.

I was born and brought up in the palace of the illustrious prince to whom my mother had the honour to be related. He was more or less the same age as myself. People urged me to be close to him, so that having known him since my childhood I should be able to enlist his support at every moment of my life. But my vanity at that time, although as yet it knew nothing of this calculation, took offence because one day during our childish games he wanted to take something away from me, and more especially he believed himself authorized by his rank to do so. I took revenge on his persistence by much-repeated blows, no consideration stopped me, and only force and violence succeeded in separating me from my adversary.

[Sade, writing this in his forties, seemed to understand something of his own nature, and was very probably telling his own story, no doubt wishing to explain it away and blaming other people for incitement. In the person of Valcour he then described how his education began and was interrupted by the declaration of war. His family were, he wrote, 'anxious to make me serve, they did not complete my education and I left for the regiment I had joined at the age when one should have been entering only the Academy'.

Sade regretted that soldiers who were too young and lacking 'a long and complete education' could not be good soldiers, but he described his own early career without any false modesty: 'The campaigns opened and I dare to state that I carried them out well. This natural impetuosity in my character, this fiery soul I had received from nature served only to give more strength and activity to that ferocious virtue called courage, one which is seen, mistakenly, no doubt, as the only one necessary to our condition.'

When Sade wrote this he had not seen a battlefield or any military scene for many years, but he had been living in a state of permanent, personal confrontation. Every day he was fighting the prison authorities and more particularly he was fighting Madame de Montreuil for not cancelling the *lettre de cachet* that kept him in prison. He had extended his enmity. He was fighting the whole of society and the only way he could do so was to use the intellectual's weapon, the pen instead of the sword. He was not an original thinker, not a great writer, but he was an aggressive, passionate man who now put all his 'natural impetuosity', his 'fiery soul', into his writing. The concept, writing and copying of *Les Cent Vingt Journées* had taken place over a few especially dark years. He had begun to see that he would need more energy to fight his way out of prison than he had needed to thrash a few women or to imagine even the 'criminal' and 'murderous' passions that were to fill the last two months of those sodomistic days.

Sade was not merely an angry middle-aged man, channelling his repressions into writing destined to console himself and shock others. He had read widely, he had been fascinated by the theatre and entertainment of all kinds, and he now began to see himself as a literary man. He wanted to entertain his potential readers while expressing his own ideas and he hoped one day he might even earn a little money. He obviously decided to follow literary fashion now, choosing the form of the epistolary novel as Rousseau had done in *La Nouvelle Héloïse* in 1761 and Laclos with the recently published *Les Liaisons Dangereuses* (1782). Rousseau, a controversial figure to the last, had died in 1771, but Sade, in his new novel, unexpectedly revived him.

His hero Valcour, after an unfortunate duel had ended in his opponent's death, has fled to Geneva, hoping to escape punishment.]

I dismissed some of my servants, having made them promise to keep the secret, and I awaited in peace what it would please heaven to decide on my behalf. It was during this painful idleness that the taste for literature and the arts replaced within my soul that frivolity, that impetuous fire which had drawn me earlier into pleasures which were both much less delightful and much more dangerous. Rousseau was living, I went to see him; he had known my family; he received me with that kindness, that frank honesty, inseparable accompaniments of genius and superior talents; he praised and encouraged the plan I was forming to renounce everything in order to dedicate myself wholly to the study of literature and philosophy; he guided my youthful mind through them and taught me to separate true virtue from the hateful structures under which it is stifled. . . .

'My friend,' he said to me one day, 'when the rays of virtue enlightened mankind, who had been too much dazzled by their brightness, they responded to this luminous flow with the prejudices of superstition, there remained to virtue no other sanctuary except deep in the hearts of honest men. Detest vice, act with fairness, love your fellow-men, enlighten them; you will be aware of virtue dwelling gently within your mind and it will console you every day for the pride of the rich and the stupidity of the despot.'

It was from the conversation of this profound philosopher, this true friend of nature and of men, that I found this dominating passion which since that time has always drawn me towards literature and the arts, and which today makes me prefer them to all the other pleasures of life, except that of adoring Aline . . . :

[Was Sade indulging in wishful thinking? Was he merely under the influence of his books, or had he really met Rousseau? He does not mention this meeting in any other documents published to date, but in *Aline et Valcour* there are several references to Rousseau's ideas, especially when Sade outlines the Utopian life of Tamoé. He also evokes the charm of the countryside when mentioning Vertfeuille, Aline's country house near Orléans, and describes how her pet dog faithfully transported letters, hidden in cakes, between the hero and heroine.

Aline and Valcour are star-crossed lovers and the reader soon grasps that nothing is likely to go right for them. Aline's father, the Président de Blamont, the brash lawyer who has made good, is determined that she should marry his friend Dolbourg, a successful if shady financier. He explains bluntly why he is not interested in any alliance with an impoverished aristocrat like Valcour.]

'I should prefer 25,000 francs a year to all those geneal-ogies which, like glow-worms, shine only in the dark, are illustrious only because one cannot see their origin and one can say anything one likes about them, for the end is missing. Valcour comes of a good family, I know; in your eyes he has an additional merit, he is passionately fond of literature; but I am very little affected by this consideration . . . I want money, and he hasn't a sou. That is his fate, inform him of it, I advise you to do so.'

[What he does not explain is his secret and sinister purpose: he wishes to control Aline's marriage because he has cast incestuous eyes on her and wants her for himself. He is intent on disposing of Valcour, and in one episode Sade chose to present Blamont as though he were a stage villain, writing entirely in dialogue interspersed with a few stage directions. In Lettre XLVI Valcour tells Aline's mother, who supports the young couple in their romantic love-affair, what happened at ten in the morning that January day in Paris. The Président de Blamont unexpectedly called on him.]

' . . . what are your feelings for my daughter?'
'Those of the deepest respect and the most inviolable love.'
'You cannot love her.'
'What law prevents me from doing so?'
'My will which is opposed to it.'
'We shall wait.'
Rising in fury: 'You will wait? So, monsieur, your entire happiness is founded on the end of my existence.'
'No, it would be gratifying to name you as my father, it would be agreeable for me to receive Aline from your hands.'
Striding up and down the room: 'Never count on that.'
'Am I wrong in that case to assure you that we shall wait? . . . A dishonest man would not tell you so.'
'But those words are telling me clearly . . .'
'They are telling you that it depends only on you to be adored as a father, or to be forgotten as an enemy.'
'It would be very diverting if a man could not dispose of his own daughter.'
'He can certainly do so as long as his attitude coincides with the happiness of this daughter.'

'These are sophistries, a father's rights over his children are not.'

[Blamont is soon tired of these discussions.]

'Monsieur de Valcour, do not force me to extremes which would make me angry; let us proceed rather by peaceful means: look (placing ten rolls of money on the table), you are not rich, I know, here are five hundred louis, sign a paper for me saying that you renounce this idea of marriage that is in your head.'

Seizing the rolls and throwing them down into the ante-chamber: 'Vile man, are you forgetting in whose house you are? Are you forgetting the baseness of your existence, the little dignity of your calling, the foulness into which your vices plunge you and all the rights granted to me by virtue and nature over your despicable self?'

'You are insulting me, monsieur.'

'In any other place I would be doing so. I content myself in my own house with requesting you to leave.'

'You are so quick-tempered!'

'And how then do I deserve to be so cruelly humiliated? Who then can make you underestimate me? Renounce for money the most precious sentiment in my life? Ignoble man, yes, I am poor, but the blood of my ancestors runs pure in my veins and I repent less of the faults which led me to lose my fortune than I would blush to possess one acquired by shameful means.'

[The impoverished aristocrat accuses the successful bourgeois lawyer of having made money by dishonest means. Blamont and his ilk, says Valcour, can compensate for the virtues they lack only 'by bags of gold whose origin they would not dare confess. The little fortune I enjoy is mine, while that of the man you offer to your daughter is the widow's dowry, the orphan's inheritance and the blood of the people'.

Blamont attempts to defend Dolbourg by explaining that he is not hopeful of any emotional response from Aline.]

'But Dolbourg has no aspirations to [her heart], he will leave her free, he will be merely pleased by this alliance, realizing fairly enough that at his age one no longer captivates the heart of a young girl: he has no aspirations to Aline's feelings, he marries her and that is all. Not every man introduces into marriage this grotesque chivalry which you display: one marries a woman for her fortune and sometimes in order to make use of her when necessary: therefore with a good or a bad grace a wife must give to her husband all the obedience she owes him; she must be blindly submissive; and moreover, whether she likes it or not, whether she is pleased or sorry to grant what one wishes and what one desires, whether it is legitimate or not . . . provided one obtains it. . . . How does all the rest affect happiness? People like you, with grand feelings, you place your happiness in metaphysical dreams which exist only in your empty heads; analyse all that, the result is nothing. I should like you to tell me what is the purpose of a woman's love, provided that one receives enjoyment from it; and at the moment of enjoyment, what does this love contribute in addition to the physical sensation?'

[Valcour protests that a virtuous woman would suffer deeply from being forced into physical intimacy with someone she does not love.]

'All that reflects the principles of young people fresh from schoolroom benches; you will see, Monsieur de Valcour, how at my age you will prefer less intellectual ideas to all these sophisms concerning love: if the husband can be happy with the physical side only, the wife should feel the same about the moral side.'

'And do you suppose that a husband can be happy without his heart being engaged?'

'I maintain that he is more so. Love is merely the thorn of enjoyment, the physical side only is the rose. . . . I should astonish you greatly if I told you that it is perhaps possible to enjoy deeper pleasures with a woman who hates us than with one who love us. The latter gives . . . with the other you have to prize the enjoyment out of her. How different is the physical sensation! In this way it always has the piquant attraction of rape, it is the fruit of victory, since one must always fight and win. It is therefore a hundred times more delightful.'

[Blamont attempts to lecture Valcour about the ignorance of young men and the unexpected advantages of growing old.]

'And what does one know at eighteen? Valuing still one's principles, believing still in virtue, admitting gods . . . dreams . . . clinging to all these prejudices, has one thought of those divine variations resulting from disgust and depravity? Has one any notion of those delightful refinements born in the midst of impotence? One has to grow old, I tell you, to be voluptuous. . . . One is a lover only when young, and it is not always Cythera where pleasure desires to worship. . . . But let us conclude, Monsieur de Valcour, I am lecturing you and I don't convince you. . . . What is your final decision?'

'To die a thousand times over rather than renounce my Aline.'

'You will bring down many misfortunes on your head.'

'If I am loved by her I shall brave them all.'

'Is that your final answer, then?'

'It is the only answer you will ever receive from me.'

And, rising in fury: 'Well, monsieur, do not be surprised at the means I shall take . . . the powers I shall employ against you.'

'If you act dishonestly you will give me the right to despise you and I shall indulge it in every respect.'

'Remember most of all, monsieur, that my house is forbidden you . . . that I shall have my daughter watched and
that if you continue to write to her or make appointments
with her I shall invoke the rigour of the law and through it I
shall make you stay within the boundaries of respect that you
owe to one of its officers.'

And he left in great anger, picking up his money-rolls and
protesting that before long my obstinacy would give me
cause for remorse.


[And so it does. The young lovers cannot defeat the schem-
ing Blamont. He arranges to have his wife poisoned and
Aline, realizing then she can escape neither her father nor
Courval, feeling unworthy of Valcour's love, kills herself.
Valcour retreats into a religious house.

Although in this long book Sade exerted some control over
his passionate wordiness he did not neglect the themes so
dear to his heart. Aline herself voices his hatred of the arranged
marriage and the way in which women were treated as chat-
tels: ' . . . so,' she said, '[a wife] is a piece of furniture that
one buys. . . . Ah! I understand, a man has her in his
bedroom like a hoard of money on his mantelpiece . . . it's a
question of making a contract, and I should be the victim of
this custom!' A far cry indeed from the position of women as
presented in *Justine*.

At the same time Sade was so anxious now to present
other aspects of his thought that he even forgot, temporarily
at least, the violent anti-clericalism in his other works. It is
an 'honest ecclesiastic' here who pleads for measures to
encourage agriculture, reduce taxes and prevent the corruption of young people by the luxury of the upper classes, 'this
pernicious luxury which ruins and upsets the rich man
without helping the poor one, quickly plunging him into the
abyss through his insane aspiration to reach what he cannot

approach without bringing about his own ruin'.

Of all Sade's major fiction, *Aline et Valcour* covers the most ground, for the tragic tale of this unhappy, heroic pair is only part of the book. This is a *roman à tiroirs*, a novel containing subsidiary novels with which the readers could divert themselves on the way. By far the longest of these, *L'Histoire de Sainville et de Léonore*, could be described as a remote sub-plot, but it is introduced by a barely credible link and is virtually a novel in its own right. The story is divided into two parts, each one recounting the adventures of two lovers who have been separated.

As Sainville searches for Léonore, who has been kidnapped in Venice, he visits two countries: Butua, situated vaguely in Africa, and Tamoé, somewhere in the South Seas. Butua, for Sade, was a Distopia, where everything disgusted his hero, while Tamoé was a Utopia, with a model civilization.]

## IN BUTUA

The prince asked who I was, and when he was told, he pointed out to me a tall white man, dried up and with a sallow skin, of about sixty-six, who, at the command of the monarch, came up to me and immediately spoke to me in a European tongue. I told this interpreter, in Italian, that I did not understand the language he was using at all. He immediately replied in good Tuscan, and we made contact with each other. This man was a Portuguese. He was called Sarmiento, captured, as I had been, about twenty years ago. He had become attached to the court and since this time had thought no more of Europe. Through him I told my story to Ben Maacoro – this was the prince's name. He had apparently wanted to know all the circumstances; I kept none from him. He laughed loudly when he was told that I braved so many perils for a woman.

'There are two thousand of them in this palace', he said,

'who wouldn't make me budge one inch. You Europeans are mad', he went on, 'to worship this sex. A woman is there to be enjoyed, and not to be adored. It is an offence against the gods of your country to give to these simple creatures the worship that is meant for them. It is absurd to grant authority to women, very dangerous to submit oneself to them; it lowers your sex, and degrades nature, when you become slaves to beings who were created to bow to our superiority.'

Without concerning myself with refuting this argument, I asked the Portuguese where the prince had acquired this knowledge about our countries.

'He judges them from what I have told him,' replied Sarmiento. 'He has never seen any Europeans except you and me.'

I asked for my liberty. The prince made me come close to him. I was naked. He examined my body. He touched it everywhere, rather in the same way as a butcher examines a cow, and said to Sarmiento that he found me too thin to be eaten and too old for his pleasures.

'For his pleasures!' I cried. . . . 'Good heavens, are there not enough women?'. . .

'It's precisely because there are too many that he is satiated with them,' the interpreter replied. . . .

'O Frenchman, do you not know then the effects of satiety? It depraves and corrupts tastes, bringing them closer to nature, while appearing to separate them. When the seed grows in the earth, when it becomes fertile and reproduces, is it by any other means than corruption, and is not corruption the first of the generating laws? When you have spent some time here, when you have known the customs of this nation, perhaps you will become more philosophical.'

'Friend,' I said to the Portuguese, 'everything that I see, and everything that you tell me, does not give me a great desire to live here. I prefer to return to Europe where they do not eat men, sacrifice girls or use boys.'

'I shall make this request on your behalf,' replied the

Portuguese, but I doubt very much if it will be granted.'

He spoke in fact to the monarch, and the reply was negative.

[Sainville did not like Butua, and planned to escape, but the prince offered him employment. He was to inspect the tribute of women who were sent regularly to the capital from all parts of the kingdom. They would always be veiled, but Sainville was to make a selection and ensure that two thousand were always available. However, he knew that the prince, Ben Maacoro, found women boring and preferred boys, whom he selected personally.]

'But at least', I said to the Portuguese, 'I flatter myself that these toothsome morsels which apparently give so much pleasure to the King will not be submitted to my inspection. I renounce the work if I have to deal with boys.'

'Have no fear,' said Sarmiento. 'He trusts his eyes only for the choice of such game. Tributes less numerous only arrive in his palace and the choice is never made by anyone except himself.'

As we talked, Sarmiento led me from room to room, and in this way I saw the whole of the palace, except the secret harems, composed of all that was most beautiful of both sexes, but where no mortal ever penetrated.

'All the prince's wives,' went on Sarmiento, 'twelve thousand in number, are divided into four classes. He forms these classes himself as he receives the women from the hands of the man who chooses them for him. The tallest, plumpest and best constituted are placed in the detachment which guards the palace. The class known as the five hundred slaves is formed of the inferior species of which I have just spoken. These women are normally from twenty to thirty years old. To them belongs the care of the interior of the palace, the work of the gardens, and generally speaking all the menial tasks. The third class he forms are from sixteen to twenty years old. They assist at the sacrifices. It is among them that the victims sacrificed to the god are chosen. The fourth class, finally, includes all that is most delicate and charming from childhood to sixteen. It is this class which serves principally his pleasures. It is here that the white women would be, if there were any . . .'

'Have there been any?' I interrupted hastily.

'Not yet,' replied the Portuguese. 'But he ardently desires some and he neglects no means which could procure some for him. . . .'

And at these words hope seemed to be reborn in my heart.

'In spite of these classifications,' went on the Portuguese, 'all these women, whatever class they belong to, do not satisfy none the less the brutality of this despot. When he wants one of them he sends one of his officers to administer a hundred strokes to the desired woman. This favour corresponds to the handkerchief of the Sultan of Byzantium, and informs the favourite of the honour which is reserved for her. She then goes where the prince awaits her, and as he often uses a great number in one day, a great number receive each morning the admonition that I have just told you about.'

'Friend', I replied at once, filled with the terrible idea that the Portuguese had just put into my head, 'the execution of this refinement of horror which you have just described will not, I hope, concern me . . .'

'No, no,' said Sarmiento, bursting into laughter, 'all that concerns the head of the seraglio. Your functions have nothing in common with his. You find him by your choice out of the five thousand women who arrive every year the two thousand from whom he chooses. When that is done you have nothing more to do with each other.'

'Good,' I replied, 'for if I had to make any one of these unfortunate women shed a single tear . . . I warn you . . . I would desert the same day. I shall do my duty with care,' I went on. 'But, entirely occupied with the woman whom I adore, these creatures will receive from me neither punishment nor favours. Thus, the privations that his jealousy imposes on me touch me very little, as you can see.'

'Friend,' the Portuguese replied, 'you seem to me to be a gallant man, you still love in the style of the tenth century. I think that I see in you one of those knights of ancient chivalry, and this virtue delights me, although I am far from adopting it. . . . We shall not see this prince again today. It is late. You must be hungry. Come and take refreshment with me. I shall finish your instruction tomorrow.'

I followed my guide. He brought me into a cottage built more or less in the taste of the prince, but infinitely less spacious. Two young negroes served supper on reed mats, and we sat in the African style. For our Portuguese, entirely denaturalized, had adopted the customs and all the ways of life in the country where he was.

They brought in a piece of roast meat, and my holy man having said his 'Benedicite' (for superstition never abandons a Portuguese), he offered me a slice from the joint which had just been placed on the table.

An involuntary movement seized me in spite of myself. 'Brother,' I said, with a distress that I could not hide, 'on the word of a European, could the dish that you serve me here not be by any chance a portion of the hips or buttocks of one of those maidens whose blood streamed earlier over the altars of your god?'

'What!' the Portuguese replied phlegmatically. 'Would such details hold you back? Do you imagine you can live here without submitting to this regime?'

'Wretched man!' I cried, getting up from the table, my gorge rising, 'your feast makes me shudder . . . I would die rather than touch it. . . . Is it then over this horrible dish that you dared to demand the blessing of heaven? Terrible man! with this mixture of superstition and crime, you did not even try to conceal your own country. . . . Go, I should have recognized you even if you had not identified yourself.'

And I was about to leave his house in terror.... But Sarmiento held me back. 'Stop,' he said. 'I forgive this shock to your habits and your national prejudices. But you abandon yourself to them too much. Stop being difficult as far as this country is concerned, and learn how to adapt yourself to situations. Repugnances are only weaknesses, my friend, they are minor illnesses of organization, whose cure you did not study when you were young, and which take possession of us when we have given in to them. It is exactly the same in this as it is in many other things: the imagination, led astray by prejudices, suggests to us first of all that we should refuse ... you make the experiment ... you find all is well and taste is sometimes adopted with just as much violence as distaste had been strong in us. I arrived here like you, full of stupid national prejudices; I found fault with everything ... I found everything absurd; the practices of these people frightened me as much as their morals, and now I do everything like them. We still belong more to habit than to nature, my friend. The latter did no more than create us, the former shapes us. It is madness to think that a moral goodness exists: every type of behaviour, absolutely different in itself, becomes good or bad depending on the country that judges it. But if he wants to live happily, the wise man should adopt that of the region where fate casts him.... In Lisbon I would probably have done like you.... In Butua I do as the negroes do.... Well, what on earth do you want me to give you for supper if you don't want to eat what everybody eats? ... I've got an old monkey there, but he'll be tough. I'll order him to be grilled for you.'

'Very well, I shall certainly eat the hind quarters of your monkey with less disgust than the fleshy bits of your king's sultanas.'

'It isn't that, good heavens! We don't eat the flesh of women. It is stringy and tasteless, and you will never find it served anywhere.'*

'This succulent dish which you despise is the leg of a Jagas killed in battle yesterday, young, fresh and whose marrow should be delicious. I had it cooked in the oven, in its own juice, look. . . . But nevertheless, allow me only, while you eat my monkey, to swallow some morsels like this.'

'Leave your monkey alone,' I said to my host as I noticed a dish of cakes and fruit which was no doubt being prepared for our dessert. 'Take your revolting supper on your own, and in a corner on the other side, as far away from you as possible, let me eat this, and I shall have much more than enough.'

'My dear compatriot,' said the cannibalized European to me, as he devoured his Jagas, 'you will recover from these fancies. I have already seen you criticize many things here which you will finish by enjoying immensely. There is nothing to which custom cannot adapt us. There is no taste which cannot come to us through habit.'

'To judge from what you say, brother, the depraved pleasures of your master have already become yours?'

'In many things, my friend. Cast your eyes on these young negroes. There are those who, as at home, teach me to do without women, and I assure you that with them I shall not be afraid of losing my pleasure. . . . If you were not so scrupulous, I would offer you some. . . . Like this,' he said, pointing to the disgusting flesh which he was eating. . . . 'But you would refuse all the same.'

---

* The most delicate, they say, is that of young boys: a German shepherd having been forced by need to eat this horrible food, continued through taste, and certified that small boy meat was better. An old woman in Brazil declared to Pinto, the Portuguese governor, exactly the same thing. St Jerome says the same thing and says that in his journey to Ireland he found this habit of eating male children established among the shepherds; they chose, he said, the fleshy parts. For these two facts stated above see the *Second Voyage of Cook*, vol. II, pages 221 and following. (Author's note)

'You may be sure of it, old sinner. Convince yourself that I would rather desert your infamous country, at the risk of being eaten by those who inhabit it, rather than remain there one moment at the cost of corrupting my morals.'

'Do not include in moral corruption the habit of eating human flesh. It is just as simple to eat a man as a cow. Say if you wish that war, the cause of the destruction of the species, is a scourge; but when this destruction is achieved, it is absolutely the same whether it is the entrails of the earth or of man which serve as a sepulchre for these disorganized elements.'

[Next day Sarmiento explains the position of women in Butua.]

'It is impossible to depict to you, my friend,' the Portuguese went on, 'in what a vile state are the women in this country. It is a luxury to have a great number of them – and the custom to make very little use of them. Both poor and rich think the same way about this question. Thus this sex fulfils in this country the same duties as our beasts of burden in Europe. It is the women who sow, plough and reap. When they come back home it is they who clean and serve, and to complete their sufferings it is always they who are sacrificed to the gods. Perpetually liable to the ferocity of this barbarous race, they are in turn victims of their bad temper, their intemperance and their tyranny. Cast your eyes over that field of maze, see these wretched naked women bent over the furrow which they are ploughing, and trembling under the whip of their husbands who lead them there. Back at the house of this cruel husband they prepare the dinner for him, serve it to him and receive without mercy a hundred strokes of the whip for the slightest negligence.'

'The population must suffer cruelly from these hateful practices?'

'For that reason it has been practically extinguished. Two strange practices add to it more than anything else. The first is the opinion of these people that a woman is impure one week before and one week after the time of the month when nature purges her. Which only leaves one week in the month when he believes her fit to serve him. The second custom, equally destructive of the population, is the rigorous abstinence to which a woman is condemned after she has had a child. Her husband sees her no more for three years. One can add to these motives for depopulation the ignominy that these people cast on the same woman once she is pregnant. From that moment she no more dares to appear, people laugh at her, they point at her and even the churches are closed to her.'

[Still searching for Léonore, hearing rumours from time to time about white women who seemed to be in captivity, Sainville travels south, seeing Dutch colonies where the settlers could hardly be distinguished from the natives 'and it was impossible to tell if they were Europeans or Hottentots'. He is well received but the language barrier prevents communication. Eventually he reaches Capetown (La Ville du Cap) and finds 'all the help I could have found in the best city of Holland'. He is alarmed by one thing. The governor, having seen Léonore's miniature, 'assured me that a woman exactly resembling the miniature that I showed him, was on board *Discovery*, the second English ship, accompanying Cook, commanded by Captain Clarke, which had just dropped anchor at the Cape'. Sainville is alarmed because the woman had said she was the wife of one of the officers. He is determined to follow the English ships, which are on their way to Tahiti, and having sailed past New Zealand, eventually finds himself, after a violent storm, on the tropical island of Tamoé. He and his crew are welcomed and conducted past the European-style fortifications at the port 'into a superb avenue with four rows of palm trees, which led from the port to the city'.

The plan of the city is circular, all the houses are identical and their façades painted in pink and green. At the centre of the city is 'a perfectly round open space surrounded with trees. Two circular buildings entirely filled this space; they were painted like the houses and only differed from them in being slightly larger and taller'.

One building is the chief's palace, the other contains public meeting-places. The circular style of the ground plan and architecture suggests that all is well in this city, there is no harsh angularity, no cruelty, unfairness or anger. Fortunately for Sainville the chief, Zamé, evidently loved by his subjects, has lived in France for three years and speaks the language. In tracing his portrait Sade obviously wanted to emphasize the contrast with the despotic rulers of France whom he hated so much.]

Great only through his virtues, respected only through his wisdom, maintained only by the wish of the people, I felt myself transported, as I saw him, into those happy times of the golden age, when kings were only the friends of their subjects, when subjects were only the children of their princes. I thought I was seeing at last Sesostris in the midst of the city of Thebes. Zamé, the name of this rare man, could have been seventy years old, he appeared barely fifty; he was tall, with a pleasant appearance, a noble bearing, a gracious smile, his eyes were bright, his forehead adorned with the finest white hair and in fact he combined the attraction of maturity with the majesty of old age.

[Over many, many pages Sainville-Sade describes the Utopian happy life on the island of Tamoé. All social customs were democratic, all attitudes were sweetly reasonable, there were no luxuries, no extremes. Women were well treated, encouraged to live in a free, natural way and to dress accordingly. Tamoé is full of surprises, and when Zamé invites Sainville to a meal he launches into a defence of vegetarianism.]

'The most wretched German princeling eats better than we do, is that not so?' Zamé said to me. 'Do you want to know why? It's because he nourishes his pride much more than his stomach, and imagines there is grandeur and magnificence in slaughtering twenty animals in order to sustain one. My vanity is concerned with different objectives: to be held dear by my fellow-citizens, to be loved by those who surround him, to do good, to prevent evil. Those are the only things, my friend, which should gratify the vanity of the man whom chance places for a moment higher than others.

'It is not through any religious principle that we abstain from eating meat; it is through regime, through humanity. Why sacrifice our brothers, when nature gives us other things? Besides, can one believe that it is good to absorb into one's entrails the putrefied flesh and blood of a thousand diverse animals? The only result of that can be a bitter chyle fluid which obviously harms our organs, weakens them, brings on infirmities and hastens death. . . . But the foods I offer you have none of these drawbacks: the vapours which their digestion sends to the brain are light, and its fibres are never disturbed as a result. You will drink water, my guest, see its limpidity, savour its cool taste; you cannot imagine the care I take to see that it is good. What liquor can equal that? Can there be any more healthy? . . . Do not ask me now why I am youthful despite my age: I have never abused my strength. . . . You will take me for a disciple of Croton. You will be very surprised to learn that I know nothing about all that and that in my life I have adopted one principle only: that of working to assemble around me the greatest possible amount of happiness, starting with the creation of happiness for others.

'I know very well that I should make further excuses to you for the bourgeois manner in which I am receiving you. A sovereign, eating with his wife and children! not paying four thousand knaves in order to have a table for monsieur, a table for madame! . . . So small-minded, such bad taste! Is not that how they would describe it in France? You can see that I know the necessary terms. O my friend! how burdensome it seems to me, how cruel it is for a sensitive soul, this intolerable luxury which comes only from the blood of the people! Do you think that I would dine, if I imagined that the gold plates on which my food is served came at the expense of my subjects' happiness, and that the feeble children of those who support this luxury could maintain their sad lives only with a few scraps of black bread kneaded in the midst of poverty, mixed with tears, sorrow and despair? . . . No, this idea would make me shudder, I could never tolerate it. What you see on my table, all the inhabitants of this island can have it on theirs, so I eat it with appetite. . . .'

[Zamé himself, and the whole structure of life on Tamoé, are too good to be true, but at least Sade put a great deal of effort into devising this tropical Utopia and creating the symbol of this virtuous democratic ruler. He was looking back to Rousseau and various other writers of his own century, adding some interpretations and advice of his own. Had *le monstre auteur* repented of his earlier behaviour and been converted into an amateur sociologist? Unlikely, but for the time being at least he had no possibility of indulging his extremist sexual tastes. He surely realized too that if and when he emerged from prison he would be too old for such indulgence: in 1784, when he was transferred to the Bastille, he was forty-four, well past middle age by contemporary standards. The writing of *Les Cent Vingt Journées de Sodome* had surely had some cathartic effect, although this was not to last. As he wrote *Aline et Valcour* Sade at least sounded calm and even 'philosophical'. All passion was not spent and his hero, Sainville, listens to the sage advice of Zamé, an amalgam of many ideas typical of the age of enlightenment and the age of the French *encyclopédistes*.]

'The natural state of man is savage life; born like the bear and the tiger in the midst of the woods, it was only in refining his needs that he thought it useful to unite in order to find more methods of satisfying them. In taking man from that condition in order to civilize him, think of his primitive state, that state of liberty for which nature formed him and add only what can perfect this happy state in which he then found himself; give him facilities, but forge him no chains; make the accomplishment of his desires easier, but do not enslave him; restrain him for his own happiness, but do not crush him through muddled and absurd laws. May all your effort tend to double his pleasures by contriving for him the art of enjoying them for a long time and in security. Give him a gentle religion like the God which forms its object; free this religion most of all from everything not concerned with faith; make it consist of deeds and not of conviction. That is how this people will cherish your administration, that is how they will subject themselves to it of their own accord and that is how in them you will have faithful friends who would die rather than abandon you or not work with you in everything that can preserve the country.'

[Some passages anticipate the man who later called himself Citizen Sade:]

'You do not wish to have beggars! Do not accumulate in the capital the streams of gold flooding in from your provinces; may everything circulate freely, and happiness, shared among all citizens, will not reveal any more one man on the heights and another in the rags of poverty. And why should some men have so much money while others do not have enough for their basic needs? You are like those children who build up all the cards they have been given into one single château. What happens? The edifice collapses. That is your situation. Your modern Babylon will crumble away like that of Semiramis, it will vanish from the earth like the flourishing cities of Greece, which were ruined only by luxury; and the State, exhausted by the embellishment of this new Sodom, will be swallowed up, like her, beneath its gilded ruins.'

[At this point a crucial footnote is added: 'It is here, as with many other passages, that we beg our readers not to forget that this work was written one year before the Revolution.'
When Sainville takes his leave of Zamé he hears a moving farewell speech.]

'Listen,' Zamé said to me with emotional enthusiasm, 'you are no doubt the last Frenchman I shall ever see. . . . Sainville, I should like to stay with this nation which gave me birth. . . . O my friend! listen to a secret that I did not want to unveil before the moment of our separation: the profound study I have made of all the governments in the world, and especially of that under which you live, have almost endowed me with the art of prophecy. By examining carefully a country, following carefully its history, ever since it has played a part on the surface of the globe, one can easily foresee what it will become. O Sainville! a great revolution is brewing in your country; the crimes of your sovereigns, their cruel extortions, their debaucheries and their ineptitude have wearied France; she is exhausted by the despotism, she is about to break its bonds. Once it has become free again, this proud part of Europe will honour with its alliance all the countries which will govern themselves in the same way as she does. . . .'

[If Sade wrote this prophetic passage before the Revolution, as he maintained, he was sending a hopeful, clairvoyant message to his readers, remembering Rousseau once again.

It is likely, however, that he inserted it later, intent on bringing his imaginative novel up to date.

While Sainville is travelling along the African coast and over the high seas in search of Léonore, she is also travelling and living through many adventures. Escaping from a convent by posing as a statue (she is nearly discovered by a pious nun), kidnapped in Venice, smuggled out of the city in a coffin, taken on board a ship that is attacked by pirates, constantly subjected to sexual blackmail, used as a pawn in a complex political game – Léonore's story is far-fetched but entertaining, especially when she meets the amoral Clémentine and the two women journey together, reacting differently from the men who try to control them. There is local colour, humour, cheerful feminist attacks on marital tyranny and male behaviour generally. Despite a few deaths and minor disasters the tone of the story is positive and the author obviously aimed at entertainment, using it as a vehicle for his various social and political messages.

Needless to say, Léonore and Sainville are reunited at the end of the story, after they have both returned separately to Europe, crossing Portugal and Spain into south-west France. Léonore has become an actress, making her début at Bayonne. She then goes to Bordeaux, where Sainville falls at her feet, they both weep with joy and so does everyone else.]

During the 1780s Sade, like his hero Valcour, was indeed *passionné des belles-lettres*, using his constant writing to express revenge, to relieve his feelings at all levels and to enlarge his personal problems into the problems of France and mankind in general. Perhaps too he had a vague hope that one day his writings would earn him some much-needed money.

In 1787 he had completed, in the space of two weeks, *Les Infortunes de la Vertu*, the first version, of novella length, of the Justine story, of which more later. He wrote other stories, some serious, some farcical, compiled a *catalogue raisonné* of his own writing to date and presumably wrote some of the many plays which he later offered to the Paris theatres, with mixed success. Altogether he had accumulated some fifteen volumes.

It was on 2nd July 1789 that Sade entered the history of the French Revolution. He is said to have made a megaphone out of a funnel that was in his cell (used for pouring water and urine out of the window: such was the sanitation in the Bastille) and shouted through it to the crowds in the rue St Antoine. He tried to tell them that the prisoners in the Bastille were being massacred. He would have known something of the first few months in the revolutionary turmoil and was determined to take part somehow in events which he claimed to have predicted, events destined to change the course of history.

The prison governor had found Sade difficult enough in the past, for he was perpetually stirring up trouble, and he acted swiftly. Two days later Sade found himself at Charenton-Saint-Maurice, just outside Paris. This establishment was a hospital for the mad, dating from the time of Louis XIV, directed by the Frères de la Charité, while the medical care was carried out by the Petits Pères. The new 'patient' soon upset the authorities there, mainly because he had been forced to leave all his papers and personal effects in the Bastille. He had asked his wife to rescue them but she had not taken action in time: his cell was ransacked, he was furious, desperate. There was some good news: in April 1790 the order was given that all prisoners held under a *lettre de cachet* must be released. So on Good Friday that year Sade left Charenton.

But there was bad news too, for when the ex-prisoner, impoverished and bereft of his writings, went to find his wife, who was living in a convent, she refused to see him. She had been loyal, understanding and faithful for years while her husband had spent the time complaining to her and about her. Sometimes he had expressed love for her, but in an unreal, theatrical kind of way which she obviously could not accept. Only two months later the couple were officially separated.

Sade had clearly become institutionalized in many ways, and he admitted to feeling 'misanthropic'. But he was not idle, the need for money constantly haunted him, especially since he now had to repay the Montreuil dowry. Fortunately he succeeded in placing some of his plays. He had always been drawn to the theatre and now the theatre changed his life: he met a young actress, Marie-Constance Quesnet, whose husband had left her and gone to America. Something of the Sade charisma had survived, for Marie-Constance was ready to attach herself to him. Early in 1791 they were living together in a house Sade had managed to buy in the one-time rue Neuve des Mathurins, and they remained together, in various locations, for the rest of his life.

There were no empty years in Sade's life, and 1791 brought several important developments. His play *Le Suborneur* was accepted by the Théâtre Italien in August, although it was not produced until two years later. On 22nd October his play *Le Comte Oxtiern ou Les Effets du Libertinage* was successfully performed at the Théâtre Molière in Paris. At the second performance, on 4th November, there was some trouble:

An incident almost upset the second performance of this play. At the beginning of the second act a discontented or hostile but certainly an indiscreet spectator shouted out: 'Lower the curtain!' This was a mistake on his part because he was not allowed to demand that the play should be stopped. The stage-hand made a mistake by obeying this isolated order and lowering the curtain more than half-way down. In the end many spectators, having had the curtain raised again, shouted 'Out with him' to the ringleader who had caused the disturbance, and they were mistaken in their turn, for they had not the right to expel a man from a play merely for having said what he felt. The result of this was a sort of split in the audience. A very small minority whistled feebly but the author was well compensated by the loud applause of the majority. They asked for the author at the end of the play: it was Monsieur de Sade.

This note appeared in *Le Moniteur*, which, after summarizing the plot, remarked that 'there is interest and energy in this play, but the part of Oxtiern is revolting in its atrociousness'.

Eight years later, with a new title, *Oxtiern ou Les Malheurs du Libertinage*, the play was acted at the theatre in Versailles. Sade himself played the part of Fabrice, and since he was as usual desperately short of money he was no doubt glad to be paid forty sols a day. The plot of *Oxtiern* is related to the story *Ernestine*, and virtue triumphs over vice. The play was published in 1800 and the story included in *Les Crimes de l'Amour*, brought out the same year by 'the author of *Aline et Valcour*'.

# La Nouvelle Justine
## ou Les Malheurs de la Vertu

In 1791 Sade brought out the first of his political pamphlets, *Adresse d'un Citoyen de Paris au Roi des Français*, but more importantly for his literary career, he arranged the clandestine publication of *Justine, ou Les Malheurs de la Vertu*.

Any reader even slightly acquainted with Sade knows that his heroine, Justine, is the unhappy girl whose continued pursuit of Good brings her nothing but suffering. She preoccupied many years of his writing life because he took her story through three or possibly four different versions. In 1787, in about two weeks, when he was still a prisoner in the Bastille, he had written a novella-length piece entitled *Les Infortunes de la Vertu* (The Misfortunes of Virtue), intending to include it in his collection *Les Crimes de l'Amour*. But the subject outgrew its original form and in 1791 he expanded it into a new and longer version entitled *Justine, ou Les Malheurs de la Vertu*. Though dedicated 'A ma bonne amie', Marie-Constance, the author remained anonymous, which was far from unusual at the time. Sade wrote to the lawyer Reinaud, stating that he had added 'spice' to the book because he needed money. He was going to deny authorship, he said, and told Reinaud not to read the book and that if it came his way he should burn it. However, he would certainly send *le roman philosophique – Aline et Valcour –* when it was available.

In his dedication to his 'good friend' Sade had concentrated on the explanation of his theme, 'one of the most sublime lessons in morality that mankind has ever received'. But this did not satisfy him. He seemed eager to express with more passion than ever his iconoclasm in all fields: religious, social, sexual. By 1797 this passion had become an obsession, almost a mania, and in *La Nouvelle Justine* of that year Sade produced an immensely long novel presenting the girl's story in a third-person narrative. The earlier versions had been recounted in the first person by the heroine herself. In all the versions of the story Justine (who had different names in the earlier ones) has an elder sister, Juliette, and at the end of *La Nouvelle Justine* the two very different girls meet again after a long separation.

Justine starts out as a girl of fourteen whose parents die (after her father's bankruptcy), leaving her, like Juliette, to make her own way in the world. Through twenty long chapters she witnesses and suffers sexual ill-treatment and torture of different kinds and is often forced into unwilling participation. At the end of each episode she either escapes from her persecutors or is driven out into a cold, harsh world only to endure more miseries. Her incurable naïvety and her belief in goodness cannot protect her against the wickedness and hypocrisy of everyone she encounters.

She has to deal with a series of villains who perpetrate crimes beyond the imagination of the average reader. In the *catalogue raisonné* of his works which he compiled in 1788 Sade writes of this book: 'There is no story of a novel in all the literature of Europe where the *genre sombre* is carried to a degree more frightening and more pathetic.'

Justine herself is frightened from the start. She has been raped by her uncle, later marked with a branding iron and is soon involved in another disaster. While hiding in a wood she sees a nobleman and his valet performing acts of sodomy.

Oh, how long this time seemed to Justine, and what a torture to virtue is the obligation to contemplate crime.

At last the scandalous actors of this scene, doubtless satisfied, stood up to return to the road that would lead them back home, when the master, approaching the bush . . . saw the tip of the kerchief swathing Justine's head.

'Jasmin,' he said to his valet, 'we are betrayed . . . we are discovered. . . . A woman . . . an impure creature has observed our mysteries. . . . Let us approach . . . let us get that whore out of there and learn the reason which put her there.'

But the trembling Justine did not give them time to drag her out of her hiding-place; she broke out of it herself, immediately. And falling at the feet of her discoverers, she exclaimed, her arms stretched out towards them: 'Oh sirs, condescend to have pity on an unfortunate whose fate is more grievous than you believe. There are very few misfortunes which can equal mine. Let not the situation in which you have found me engender any suspicion about myself – it is the result of poverty rather than of my sins. Far from increasing the evils which overwhelm me, pray diminish them by making it easy for me to escape the torments which pursue me.'

Monsieur de Bressac – such was the name of the young man into whose hands Justine had fallen – amply endowed with wickedness, was not supplied with a very abundant stock of commiseration. It is, unfortunately, only too common to see luxuriousness extinguish pity in the hearts of men. Its ordinary effect is to harden; whether because the great majority of man's deceits necessitate apathy of the soul, or the violent shock this passion produces upon the majority of nerves diminishes the strength of their action, it is still a fact that the libertine is rarely a man of sensitivity.*

But in Bressac, further to this hardness, natural to the type

* And that for the sole reason that sensitivity proves weakness, and libertinage strength. (Author's note)

of persons we are speaking of, there was coupled a profound disgust for women . . . such an inveterate hatred for all which is characteristic of the sex – which he called INFAMOUS – that Justine would have had great difficulty in successfully evoking in him those sentiments which it was her concern to inspire.

'Well, my little dove,' said Bressac to her, coldly, 'if you are looking for dupes, try better company. Neither I nor my friend ever touch women. They are horrible in our eyes and we carefully avoid them. If it is alms you are after, try people who like good deeds – we perform only bad ones. But tell me, wretch, did you see what passed between this young man and myself?'

'I saw you talking on the grass,' said the prudent Justine. 'Nothing else, sirs, I swear.'

'I should like to believe it,' said Bressac, 'and for your sake. If I thought you had seen anything else you would never leave that bush. . . . Jasmin, it is early yet, we have time to hear this girl's story. Let us listen, and afterwards we shall see what needs to be done.'

The young men sat down: Justine placed herself beside them, and related to them with her usual frankness all the misfortunes which had oppressed her since her arrival in this world.

'Come Jasmin,' said Bressac, getting to his feet, 'let us for once be just. Equitable Themis has condemned this creature. Do not let us allow the designs of this goddess to be so cruelly frustrated. Let us make the delinquent suffer the death sentence she would have undergone. This petty murder, so far from being a crime, will only be a reparation in the moral order. Since we sometimes have the misfortune to disturb it, let us, when the opportunity arises, re-establish it bravely.'

And the cruel man lifted the unfortunate girl from the ground and began to drag her towards the centre of the wood, laughing at her tears and cries.

'First of all, let us undress her,' said Bressac, tearing away all the veils of decency and modesty, without the attractions that this operation revealed to him in any way softening a man hardened to all the wiles of a sex that he despised. 'What a nasty creature is a woman,' he said, rolling her over and over on the ground with his foot. 'Oh, Jasmin! . . . The ugly creature!' Then he spat on her and asked: Tell me, my dearest, would you enjoy this creature?'

'Not even from the arse,' said the valet.

'Well, and yet that's what stupid men call their divinity; that's what those idiots adore. . . . Look, look at this body pierced in front . . . look at this disgusting cunt; that's the temple where absurdity makes its sacrifice; there is the workshop of human regeneration. Come, no pity! Let's tie up this wretch. . . .

And immediately the poor girl was bound to a tree with a rope these monsters made out of their cravats and handkerchiefs: then they placed her between four trees, one limb firmly attached to each; and in this cruel position, which let her stomach hang down without support towards the ground, her suffering was so intense that a cold sweat dripped from her forehead; she existed then only through the violence of the torment; if they stopped compressing her nerves she would die. The more this wretched girl suffered, the more the young men seemed to find the spectacle entertaining. They gazed at her with delight; they watched eagerly every time her face was contorted by her burning anguish and the more violent her reactions the greater was their ghastly pleasure.

'That's enough,' said Bressac. 'I agree, this time, her fear is punishment enough. Justine,' he continued, untying her bonds and ordering her to get dressed, 'keep a discreet tongue, and follow us. If you attach yourself to me, you will have no cause to repent of it. My mother needs a second woman. I shall present you to her, and on the truth of your story, I shall answer to her for your conduct. But if you abuse my kindness, betray my confidence, or refuse to submit to my intentions, then, Justine, look at these trees. Examine the ground they overhang, which would become your burial place, and remember that this unhappy spot is but a league from the château to which I am taking you, and that at the slightest transgression on your part you will be brought back here immediately.'

The flimsiest sign of happiness is to the unfortunate what the restorative dew of the morning is to the flower dried up the day before by the burning fires of the sun. In tears, Justine cast herself at the feet of her seeming protector, swearing to be obedient and to conduct herself well. But the barbarous Bressac, as insensible to this dear child's joy as to her grief, said to her coldly: 'We shall see . . .' and they set off.

Jasmin and his master spoke together in whispers. Justine followed them humbly without saying a word. An hour and a quarter was enough to bring them to the château of Madame de Bressac – the luxury and magnificence of which showed Justine that whatever post might be destined for her in this house, it could surely be only advantageous to her if the malevolent hand that had never ceased to torment her did not reappear to trouble the flattering prospects that seemed to be opening up before her eyes.

Half an hour after his arrival the young man presented her to his mother.

Madame de Bressac was a woman of forty-five, still beautiful, respectable and sensitive, but astonishingly severe concerning morals. Vainglorious of the fact that she had never made one false step all her life, she did not forgive any weakness in others, and by this extreme severity, far from earning the tenderness of her son, she had, so to speak, repelled him from her bosom. Bressac had many faults, it is agreed. But where should indulgence build her temple if not in a mother's heart? A widow since the death of the young man's father two years before, Madame de Bressac possessed an income of 100,000 écus, which, joined with the provision more than twice as great from the fortune of his father, would one day assure our villain, as can be seen, an annual revenue of nearly a million. Despite such great expectations Madame de Bressac gave her son little; would an allowance of 25,000 francs be sufficient to pay for his pleasures? There is nothing so expensive as this kind of enjoyment. Men, it is agreed, cost less than women, but the lewd acts one relishes with them are repeated more often; one is much more fucked against than fucking.

Nothing had been able to bring the young Bressac to service. Everything which distracted him from his debauchery was so insupportable in his eyes that he could not suffer its bond.

For three months of the year Madame de Bressac lived on the estate where Justine first met her; the remainder of the time she spent in Paris. During this three months of country life, however, she insisted that her son should never leave her. A cruel punishment for a young man who detested his mother, and regarded as lost every moment spent away from the city that was for him the centre of pleasure!

[Madame de Bressac, having heard and verified Justine's story, engages her as a maid and the girl becomes attached to her. Unfortunately she also becomes attached to her son. Sade was interested enough in this character to depict him in more detail than he usually gave in his descriptions of men, and he also brought him back into Justine's story at a later stage. It has even been suggested that Bressac was not unlike Sade himself: if, that is, one accepts the theory that he was either homosexual or bisexual.]

To the charm of his youth, Bressac enjoined a most attractive appearance. If his features or his figure had any faults, it was because they came somewhat close to that nonchalance . . . that softness, which belongs only to women.

It seemed as if nature, in bestowing on him the attributes of that sex, had inspired him equally with its tastes. But what a soul was buried beneath these feminine attractions! It contained every vice that characterized those of the greatest criminals. Nowhere were there such extremes of malice, vengeance, cruelty, atheism, debauchery, utter neglect of all duties and principally of those which less powerfully constituted souls seemed to make their delights. This singular young man's prime mania was to detest royally his mother, and unfortunately this hatred, based on his principles, was nourished within him both on arguments that permitted no reply and also on the powerful interest that he must inevitably have had in getting rid of her as soon as possible. Madame de Bressac did her best to guide her son back to the path of virtue; but in this she showed herself too strict. The result was that the young man, more excited by the effects of this truth, simply abandoned himself with greater recklessness to his tastes, and from her endeavours the poor woman only gathered a harvest of hatred that was infinitely stronger.

[Bressac hated his mother, told Justine that he alone had helped her and assured her that he did not want the usual favours from her, because he was not interested in women. He hinted that he wanted other kinds of service.]

Such speeches, frequently repeated, seemed so obscure to Justine that she did not know how to reply to them. She did so, nevertheless, and perhaps rather too forcefully. Must it be confessed? Alas! yes. To disguise Justine's faults would be to deceive the confidence of the reader, and to be ungrateful for the interest that her misfortunes have up till now evoked.

However unworthy Bressac's actions with regard to her may have been, from the first day she had seen him, she had been unable to defend herself against a violent feeling of affection for him. Gratitude increased in her heart this involuntary desire to which every day new strength was lent by the perpetual encounters with the cherished object: Justine definitely adored this blackguard, despite herself, with the same ardour that she idolized her God, her religion . . . virtue. A thousand times she had reflected to herself upon the cruelty of this man, his antipathy to women, the depravity of his tastes and the moral gulf that separated them; and nothing in the world could extinguish this budding passion. If Bressac had asked her for her life, had desired her to shed her blood, Justine would have given it, lavished it, and been heartbroken that she could not yet of her own free will make greater sacrifices to the sole object of her passion. Such is love, and that is why the Greeks portrayed him with his eyes bandaged. But Justine said not a word, and the ungrateful Bressac was far from discerning the cause of the tears she shed daily on his behalf. It was very difficult, however, while he was in no doubt about the desire she had to anticipate everything which could please him, not to realize that her attentions were strong enough and blind enough to serve even his misdeeds as far as decency would permit, and the care she always took to disguise them from his mother. By this conduct, so natural in a heart stricken with love, Justine had deserved young Bressac's entire confidence; and everything coming from this cherished lover seemed of so great price in Justine's eyes that very often the poor girl imagined that she obtained from love what was, in fact, bestowed upon her from debauchery . . . wickedness, or perhaps more certain still, the need that he thought he had of her for the dreadful projects in his heart.

[She is horrified when she heard what these projects are: he wants her to 'warm up' the boys he uses for sex, and later, worse still, much worse, he explains that he wants her to help him kill his mother. (In earlier versions of the story Bressac was concerned with killing his aunt. Sade had now deepened his crime.) The young man then takes on the author's voice.]

'I am well aware of your repugnance, but since you are intelligent, I flattered myself I could conquer it and prove to you that this crime which appears so enormous to you is at bottom merely a very simple affair.

'Two crimes offer themselves here to your too-unphilosophical eyes, Justine: the destruction of a creature resembling oneself, and the evil with which, according to you, this destruction is increased when this creature belongs so closely to one. With regard to the crime of destroying a fellow-man, be quite certain, dear girl, that it is purely illusory. . . . But the creature that I shall destroy is my mother. It is in this respect that we shall examine this murder.

'There can surely be no doubt that the pleasure expected by the mother from the conjugal act is the sole motive which impels her to it. This fact being established, I ask you how gratitude can be born in the heart of the fruit of this selfish act? Did the mother, in abandoning herself to it, work for herself or for her child? I do not think that such a thing can be in any doubt. However, the child is born, the mother suckles it. Is it in her second operation that we are to discover the motive we seek for the sentiment of gratitude? Certainly not. If the mother renders her child this service, do not doubt but that she is activated only by the natural sentiment that impels her to relieve herself of a secretion that otherwise could become dangerous to her. She is imitating the female animals which, like her, the milk would kill, if, like them, she were not immediately relieved of it by this process. Now, can either of them be relieved of it other than by letting it be sucked by the animal that desires it and that by another natural movement equally reaches for the breast? . . . Here then is the child, born and nourished, without our having discovered in either of these two operations any reason for gratitude towards her who gave him life and maintains it in him. Would you speak to me of the cares that follow those of infancy? Ah, see in them no other motives than those of the mother's pride. In this case unspeaking nature no more demands them from her than she does from other female animals. Beyond the attentions necessary to the child's life and the mother's health, a mechanism no more extraordinary than that of the marriage of the vine to the elm, beyond these attentions, I say, nature decrees nothing more. . . . It is from habit and vanity that women prolong maternal cares; and far from being useful to the child, they weaken his instinct, degrade him, and cause him to lose his power. You would say that he always needs to be led. I ask you now if this child should consider himself bound by gratitude because the mother continues to undertake attentions that he can do without and which only benefit her? What? Should I owe someone something because that person has done for me what I could do perfectly well without, and which only the other needs? You will agree that such a mode of thought would be a ghastly extravagance. And so the child has now reached the age of puberty without our having found in him the slightest reason for gratitude towards his mother. What would be the result of his reflections if he then made any? Dare I say it. . . . To him she has transmitted her infirmities, the bad qualities of her blood, her vices, and finally an existence that he has received only in order to be unhappy. Are there any very great motives for gratitude there, I ask you? . . .

'Compare all the other so-called duties of man towards his mother; measure them all by these reflections, and then give your judgement upon your alleged duties towards your father, your wife, your husband, your children, etc. Once you are thoroughly imbued with this philosophy, you will see that you are alone in the universe, that all the chimerical links that have been forged for you are the work of men, who, naturally born weak, seek to stay themselves with these bonds. A son believes he has need of his father; the father, in his turn, imagines he has need of his son. That is the cement of these alleged ties, these sacred duties. But I defy anyone to find them in nature. So leave your prejudices there, Justine, and serve me: your fortune is made.'

'Oh sir,' replied the poor girl, quite terrified, 'this indifference that you suppose exists in nature is still nothing but the result of your mind's sophistries. Listen instead to your heart, and you will hear it condemn all these false arguments of vice and debauchery. This heart, to whose tribunal I ask you to refer, is it not in fact the sanctuary in which this nature that you outrage wishes you to listen to and worship her? If she engraves in it the strongest horror for the crime that you contemplate, will you grant me that it is to be condemned? I know that at the moment you are blinded by passions; but as soon as their voices are still, to what an extent remorse will make you unhappy! The more active your sensitivity, the more the needle of repentance will torment you. Oh sir, cherish and respect the remaining years of this tender and precious friend. Do not sacrifice her, you will perish of despair. Every day, at every moment, you will see before your eyes this adored mother whom your blind fury has consigned to the tomb. You will hear her beseeching voice whisper again the soft words that were the joy of your childhood. She will appear to you at night, she will torment you in your dreams: with her bleeding hands she will open the wounds with which you have mutilated her. From then onwards not one happy moment will shine for you in this world; all your pleasures will be spoilt, all your thoughts troubled; a heavenly hand, whose power you misprize, will avenge the days you have destroyed by poisoning all your own. And without having enjoyed your hideous crimes you will perish of the mortal regret of daring to accomplish them.'

Justine wept as she spoke these last words; she was on her knees at the feet of this ferocious man who listened to her with an air blended of rage and contempt. She begged him by all that was most sacred to him to forget an infamous project that she swore to conceal all her life. But she did not know the monster with whom she was dealing. She did not know to what an extent the passions bolster and fortify crime in such a soul as Bressac's. She did not know that all the promptings of virtue and sensibility in such circumstances were like so many needles in the scoundrel's heart, whose sharp pricks invested the projected atrocity with even greater violence. The true libertine loves even the dishonour, the scars, the censures that are the deserts of his execrable action. They are delights to his perverse soul. Have we not seen the man who loves even the tortures that human vengeance prepares for him, who undergoes them joyfully, who regards the scaffold as a throne of glory on which he would be most grieved not to perish with the same courage that had animated him in the loathsome exercise of his sins and outrages? There you see the man in the last degree of considered corruption: there you see Bressac.

He stood up, coldly. 'I can see', he said to Justine, 'that I was deceived. I am more sorry for you than for myself. No matter, I will find other means, and you will have lost much, without your mistress gaining anything.'

Such a threat changed all Justine's ideas. By not accepting the crime proposed to her, she risked a lot on her own account, and her mistress would still inevitably die. By agreeing to take part, she protected herself from Bressac's wrath, and would certainly save the marquise. This reflection which was the work of an instant in her, determined her to accept everything, but as so quick a change of front would inevitably have given rise to suspicion of deceit, she made the most of her pretexts for some time, and put Bressac in the position of frequently repeating his maxims to her. Gradually she gave the impression of not knowing any more what to reply. Bressac believed her converted and threw himself into her arms. What enjoyment for Justine if this movement had been motivated by wisdom! . . . But the time for that had passed; this man's horrible conduct, his parricidal designs, had extinguished every affection nourished in this poor girl's weak heart. And now, calmly, she saw in the former idol of her heart only a criminal, unworthy of reigning there for even a single instant.

'You are the first woman I have kissed,' said Bressac, embracing her ardently. 'You are delicious, my child. Has a ray of philosophy penetrated your mind, then? Is it possible that so charming a head could have remained shrouded for so long in terrible prejudices! . . . Oh Justine! the torch of reason is now dispersing the shadows into which superstition had plunged you. You see clearly, you can picture the nullity of crime, and at last the sacred duties of personal interest prevail over the frivolous considerations of virtue. Come, you are an angel, I do not know why it is you do not instantly make me change my tastes.'

[Bressac tries to poison his mother, but Justine gives him away. He then abuses his mother sexually, with the help of two valets and the unwilling participation of Justine. Finally he has his mother attacked by four huge dogs but found to be still alive, he]

. . . placed a dagger in Justine's hand, seized the arm which held this weapon, and guided it, despite all the unfortunate girl's resistance, into the heart of the unhappy lady, who died imploring God's pardon on her son.

'Do you see the murder you have just committed,' said the barbarous Bressac to the almost unconscious Justine who was soaked in the blood of her mistress. 'Look, can there be, anywhere in the world, a more shocking act? You shall be punished for it, you must be. You shall be broken alive on the wheel, you shall be burnt.'

Pushing her into the adjoining room, he locked her in, first placing beside her the bloody dagger. Then he opened up the château, mimicking grief and tears, saying that a fiend had just assassinated his mother, that he had found the weapon in the criminal's room, and held her prisoner, while he quickly demanded every assistance from justice. But this time a protecting God saved innocence. The measure had not been filled, and it was to be with other experiences that Justine must accomplish her destiny. In his confusion, Bressac believed he had firmly locked the door. He had not, and Justine profited from the moment when everyone was gathered in the courtyard of the château, to leave rapidly, escaping by the gardens to find the gate of the park half open, and thence into the forest.

[Justine, now seventeen years old, next finds herself in the house of a villainous doctor named Rodin, who runs an establishment regarded in the area as a school. Justine thinks she is being engaged for a good reason because he is a widower with a daughter of fourteen who needs a companion. She does not of course know that his principal sexual partner is his sister Célestine, who prefers women but accepts anal sex with men. Sade explains the situation in a footnote: 'Nearly all tribads are like this. In imitating the passions of men, they relish their refinements, and since that of sodomy is the most refined of all, it is quite obvious that they make it one of their most divine pleasures.'

Neither does Justine know that the so-called school is merely a centre of libertinage. Rodin's daughter, Rosalie, explains the situation. Justine not only resists Rodin's attempts to seduce her through an impassioned speech on the uselessness of virtue, but she persuades Rosalie to become a Christian and even introduces a priest into the house.

Rodin's iniquity reaches its height when he attempts sexual intercourse with his daughter while performing a hysterectomy on her, assisted by a doctor colleague, his sister and, as usual, the unwilling Justine. Rosalie of course dies and Rodin's colleague, Rombeau, suggests how they might conclude this lethal orgy: 'The pleasure of killing a woman soon passes; after she is dead she no longer feels anything; the delights of making her suffer disappear with her life; there remains only the memory. Let us do better,' Rombeau continued, putting an iron in the fire, 'let us punish her a thousand times more than if we were robbing her of her life.'

Justine is then branded on her shoulder, like a common criminal, beaten, sexually abused and turned out into the surrounding forest. She is eighteen now, and Sade makes a point of saying that in spite of everything she has suffered she is now more attractive than ever: ' . . . her figure was better developed, her hair thicker and longer, her skin fresher and more appetizing; and her breasts, treated carefully by people who were not much attracted by this part of her body, had filled out more roundly. Justine, therefore, was a very beautiful girl, a creature well capable of arousing in libertines the most violent . . . the most abnormal . . . the most lascivious desires'.

Nothing seems less credible, but Sade had to keep his story going. He did so by detailing Justine's disastrous adventures among a group of villainous monks, who run a kind of brothel for boys and girls. One of them relates his own unedifying story at length, for Sade would miss no opportunity of attacking clerics at any level. Justine escapes from the Abbaye de Sainte-Marie-des-Bois and at once falls into another dangerous place, an 'inn', wrote Sade in his chapter heading, 'where travellers will do well not to stop'. The inn is run by the d'Esterval couple who do not need money but need to satisfy their 'execrable inclinations'. They will kill any visitors by an ingenious trap which lowers the bedroom floors into the cellars, and it is now Justine's task to warn the visitors, without giving away any details. They all perish, but one evening an unexpected guest rides up. It is the man Justine had admired until he killed his mother and accused her of the murder. It is Bressac. He turns out to be a close relative of d'Esterval, but the innkeeper is not prepared to let him stay alive. Thanks to Justine, however, he survives, and Bressac admits that he has been guilty of the matricide. He is on his way to stay with his uncle, Gernande, and easily persuades the d'Estervals to accompany him. Justine has no choice, she has to go too.

Although it is hard to choose which of Sade's loathsome men is the most dastardly of all, Gernande is a strong candidate. His hobby is to bleed his victims, especially his current wife, until they reach death's door, and then abuse them until they pass through it. He has always felt murderous towards women whom he has married, and as soon as one wife is dead he at once acquires a new one. Soon after the d'Estervals and Bressac have joined this blood-soaked house-party the group is augmented by more relations, including one particularly nauseating adolescent boy who specializes in incestuous sexual attacks of all kinds.

Gernande is nothing if not extreme, and Sade allowed himself a moment of self-indulgence by describing the Gargantuan eating habits of this monster. He welcomes his nephew, Bressac, and the d'Estervals, who are cousins of his, although he had never met them before. He is thrilled by the stories of their wickedness and looks forward to the orgies they will share, but in the meantime he will keep to his routine.]

'I hear the dinner-bell; let us go to table. This is an interesting time for me; when the table is cleared I shall be all yours; it's my moment; we shall then carry out a few scenes which will please all of us.'

They went to table.

'Forgive me,' said the count, 'I was not expecting you, my

nephew had not written to me. I shall be giving you my everyday dinner, please accept its mediocre quality.'

Two soups were served: one with Italian pasta and saffron, the other a fish soup with a coulis of ham; the middle course was a sirloin of beef, English style; twelve hors-d'oeuvres, six of them cooked and six from the kitchen garden; twelve entrées, including four with meat, four with poultry and four with pastry; a boar's head accompanied by twelve dishes of roast meat, along with ranges of entremets, twelve consisting of vegetables, six of different creams and six of patisserie; twenty dishes of fruit, fresh or cooked; six varieties of ice; eight kinds of wine, six different liqueurs, rum, punch, spirits of cinnamon, chocolate and coffee. Gernande broached all the dishes; some or them were wholly consumed by him; he drank twelve bottles of wine: four bottles of Volnay, to start with, four from Ai, with the roast; the Tokay, the Paphos, the Madeira and the Falernian were drunk with the fruit; Gernande finished with two bottles of West Indian liqueur, a pint of rum, two bowls of punch and ten cups of coffee. The d'Estervals and the Marquis de Bressac, who were just as big eaters, had kept up with him, but they seemed intoxicated, whereas Gernande was as fresh as if he had just awakened. As for Justine, who had been allowed to sit at the end of the table, she revealed restraint, sobriety, much modesty. Those were the habitual virtues she constantly opposed to the vulgar intemperance of all the criminals among whom her unhappy destiny placed her.

[Sade was known to be both gourmet and gourmand; after so many years in prison without exercise he had grown very fat. It has sometimes been suggested that he used some of his own characteristics in describing Gernande, but their shared love of food is harmless enough. As for Justine, her destiny is not as unhappy as that of Gernande's wife, whom she befriends and intends to help. But temporarily at least she forgets her 'habitual virtue' and escapes.

Justine now spends some time with a gang of well-organized professional beggars who live in a series of underground caves. She leaves them after refusing to act as a procuress for an elderly merchant in Lyon whose sexual taste involves a form of blasphemy. Walking towards Vienne she sees a man being viciously trampled to death by two horsemen. She goes to his aid, the victim recovers, thanks her and then takes her to his château where, he says, his sister needs a servant. Justine soon realizes her mistake. This man, Roland, is a manufacturer of counterfeit money and he is also as villainous as the other men to whom Justine naïvely entrusted herself. His cruelty towards her is all the more horrible because he forces her to take an active part in it and engineers his sexual tortures in such a way that she experiences orgasm. However, when Roland attempts to kill her, while *he* experiences orgasm, Justine is skilful enough to survive.]

Roland, whom it is essential to describe before bringing him on stage, was a short, thickset man, aged thirty-five, incredibly strong, as hairy as a bear, with a dark face, a fierce expression, his skin very brown, his features male and pronounced, with a long nose and a beard growing up to his eyes, his eyebrows black and heavy, his prick so long, so inordinately huge, that Justine had never seen anything like it. In addition to this somewhat repulsive physique our producer of counterfeit louis possessed all the vices that can result from a fiery temperament, much imagination and an affluence too considerable for him to have suffered any great problems. Roland was completing his fortune: his father, who had begun to accumulate it, had left him very rich and as a result this young man had already lived a full life. He had become blasé about ordinary pleasures, he now had recourse only to horrors; they alone succeeded in satisfying desires exhausted by over-indulgence. The women who served him were all employed in his secret debaucheries; and, in order to satisfy slightly less dishonourable pleasures in which this libertine could none the less find the savour of crime which delighted him more than anything, Roland had his own sister as mistress; it was with her that he finally extinguished the passions that he had recently ignited with others.

He was almost naked when he came in; his face, which was highly inflamed, revealed both the proofs of his recent excesses at the table and the abominable lust which devoured him. For a moment he contemplated Justine with eyes that made her shudder.

'Take off those clothes,' he said, tearing off the ones she had put on to wear during the night, 'yes, take all that off and follow me. I made you aware yesterday of the risks you would run if you abandoned yourself to laziness. But if you should want to betray us, since that crime would be much greater, the punishment must match it: so come and see what it would be like.'

Seizing her at once by the arm, the libertine drew her after him. He led her by his right hand; in his left he carried a small lantern which lit their way with a feeble light. After several detours they reached the door to a cellar. Roland opened it; and, making Justine walk in front of him, he told her to go down while he fastened this door again. A hundred steps further down was a second door which was opened and closed in the same way; but after this one there was no more stairway: there was a narrow path cut out from the rock, and very steep. Roland said not a word. This alarming silence redoubled Justine's terror and since she was totally naked she was even more keenly aware of the horrible humidity of these subterranean depths. To the right and left of the pathway she was following were several niches with coffers containing the riches of these evildoers. Finally they came to the last door, made of bronze; it was more than eight hundred feet down in the bowels of the earth. Roland opened it and the girl who was following him fell back as she saw the ghastly place into which she was being led.

Roland, seeing her weaken, pulled her up and pushed her roughly into the middle of a circular vault where the walls, hung with funeral palls, were decorated with only the most gruesome objects. Skeletons of all ages and sexes, interspersed with strings of bones, death's heads, snakes, toads, bundles of rods, sabres, daggers, pistols and totally unknown weapons. Such were the horrors that could be seen on the walls, lit only by a three-wick lamp hanging from one corner of the vault. From the archway a rope eight feet long hung down to the ground and, as you will soon see, was there only to play a part in horrible killings. To the right was a coffin propped open by the spectral figure of Death, armed with a threatening scythe. Beside this was a prie-dieu and a little beyond could be seen a table, on it a crucifix between two black tapers, a dagger with three hooked blades, a pistol ready cocked and a cup full of poison. To the left was the body of a recently dead, superbly beautiful woman, attached to a cross; she had been placed face downwards, revealing an ample view of her buttocks . . . but they had been cruelly mauled; there were still long, thick nails in the flesh; and drops of black congealed blood formed scabs all down her thighs; she had the most beautiful hair in the world; her lovely head was turned towards the front and seemed to beg for mercy. Death had in no way disfigured this sublime creature; and the delicacy of her features, affected less by decay than by sorrow, offered still the absorbing spectacle of beauty in despair. The depths of the vault were filled by a huge black sofa from where all the atrocities of this place could be seen.

'This is where you will die, Justine,' said Roland, 'if you ever conceive the fatal idea of leaving this establishment. Yes, it's here that I shall come myself to put you to death . . .

there that I shall make you suffer mortal anguish by the harshest methods I can find.'

As he pronounced this threat Roland grew inflamed; his agitation and disorder made him resemble a tiger ready to devour his prey. It was then that he took out into the daylight the fearsome member with which he was equipped.

'Have you ever seen anything like this?' he asked, making Justine take hold of it. 'Even as it is,' this faun went on, 'it must all the same enter into the narrowest part of your body, even if I have to cleave you in two. My sister, who is much younger than you, tolerates it in the same place. Never do I enjoy women in any different way. Therefore it must tear you apart also.'

'Yes, it's in there, in there, that I shall drive in this member which frightens you. It will enter up to its entire length. It will tear your anus. It will make you bleed; and I shall be in a state of intoxication.'

He was in a rage as he spoke these words, mingled with curses and odious blasphemies. The hand touching the temple he apparently wished to attack strayed all over the adjacent parts; he punched them, he scratched them; he attacked her breast in the same way and bruised it so deeply that Justine suffered terrible pain for two weeks afterwards. He then placed her on the sofa, rubbed all her pubic hair with spirits of wine, set fire to it and burnt it all away; his fingers seized hold of her clitoris, and crushed it roughly; he then inserted them inside and his nails mauled the membrane which lined it. Containing himself no longer he told Justine that since he had her in his lair she might as well never leave it, that would save him the trouble of coming down again. . . . Our wretched girl threw herself to her knees, she dared to remind him again of the service she had done him and soon realized that she was making him angry by speaking of the rights to his pity she imagined herself deserving from him.

'Be quiet!' this monster told her as he pushed her over with a fierce blow from his knee in the hollow of her stomach. 'Come on,' he continued, pulling her up by the hair, 'come on, get ready, you hussy! I'm certainly going to kill you.'

'Oh, sir!'

'No, no, you must die: I don't want to hear you reproach me any more over the small services you did for me. I don't want to owe anything to anybody. Other people must owe everything to me. You're going to die, I tell you. Get into this coffin, so that I can see if you can fit into it.'

He stretched her out in it . . . he fastened her in and left the vault. Justine believed she was lost; never had death come close to her in more certain and more hideous forms. However, Roland reappeared; he took her out of the coffin.

'You would be very comfortable there,' he told her. 'This bier might have been made for you. But letting you come to an end there quietly would be too good a death. I'm going to make you feel one of a different kind which is not without its pleasures. Go on, pray to your blasted God, you trollop! Beg him to hasten and avenge you, if he really has the power to do so. . . .'

The wretched girl threw herself on the prie-dieu and as she opened her heart aloud to the Eternal, Roland redoubled his harassments and tortures on the posterior parts that she was exposing to him. He flagellated them with all this strength, using a whip armed with steel spikes, and each blow from it caused blood to spurt up to the roof.

'Well,' he went on, with blasphemous words, 'your God isn't helping you. So that's how he leaves unhappy virtue to suffer? He abandons it into the hands of crime! Ah! what a God, Justine, what a God that is . . . what an infamous confounded God! How I despise him and cheerfully reject him! Come,' he then said, 'your prayer must be finished! Is so much needed for an abominable God who fails to hear you?'

As he spoke these words he placed her on the edge of the

sofa which formed the back of this sepulchral place:

'I've told you, Justine,' he went on, 'you must die.'

He seized hold of her arms, bound them over the small of her back, then he passed round the victim's neck a cord of black silk. The two ends, which he held, could be tightened at will, they could compress the victim's breathing and send her into the other world in the longest or shortest time, as it suited him.

'This torment is more pleasant than you might think, Justine,' said Roland. 'You will be aware of death only through inexpressible sensations of pleasure. As this cord tightens over your nerve centres, it will inflame the organs of sexual enjoyment. The result is certain. If all the people condemned to this torture knew the degree of pleasure in which it causes death, they would be less frightened of this punishment for their crimes, they would commit them more often and with more confidence. What human being would hesitate to enrich himself at the expense of others when, in addition to the near-certainty of not being found out, his only fear, if he should be discovered, would be the total certainty of the most delightful of deaths? This delightful operation,' Roland went on, 'compressing in the same way the place where I shall position myself' (and in saying this he got ready to bugger her) 'will also double my pleasure.'

But his efforts were in vain: in vain did he prepare the way in, in vain did he open it up and moisten it, he was too monstrously proportioned to succeed and his endeavours were constantly repulsed. Then his fury knew no bounds; his finger-nails, his hands, his feet helped him to take revenge on the resistance opposed to him by nature. He took up his position again; the fiery sword slid to the edge of the nearby channel; and from the force of the impact he penetrated more than half way down. Justine uttered a terrible cry. Roland, infuriated by his mistake, withdrew in a rage, and this time he struck at the other entrance with so much force that the moistened dart plunged into it and tore the edges. Roland took advantage of this first shock; his efforts became more violent; he gained some terrain. As he advanced, the fatal cord that he had passed round Justine's neck tightened. She uttered frightful screams. The ferocious Roland, diverted by this, forced them to redouble. Since he was over-confident of their futility, and too sure of stopping them when he wanted to, he became inflamed by their shrill sounds. But he was soon to be overtaken by intoxication; the tightening of the cord affected the degree of his enjoyment. Gradually the unfortunate girl's cries became fainter: the cord then became so tight that her senses weakened, although she did not lose her sensitivity. She was rudely shaken by Roland's enormous member tearing at her entrails. Despite her appalling state she felt herself flooded with jets of sperm from the horrifying man who was buggering her; she heard the cries he uttered as he spilled it. A moment of insensibility followed; but she was soon freed, her eyes opened again to the light and her organs seemed to expand.

'Well, Justine,' said her executioner, 'I swear that if you are truthful you have felt only pleasure.'

Unfortunately nothing was more certain; our heroine's cunt was completely soaked and proved that Roland's assertion was true. For a moment she tried to deny it.

'Whore,' said the villain, 'do you think you can impress me, when I can see what is flooding your vagina? You have discharged, the result is inevitable.'

'No, sir, I assure you!'

'Well, little do I care! You must, I imagine, know me well enough to be quite certain that your pleasure in what I undertake with you concerns me infinitely less than mine. And this pleasure I seek was so intense that I'm going to enjoy it once again. Now, Justine,' said Roland, 'your life will depend only on you.'

He then passed round the wretched girl's neck the rope

that hung down from the roof. As soon as it was tightly in place he tied a string to the stool on which Justine had climbed, he held the other end and went to sit in an armchair facing her. In one of the victim's hands was a sickle, its blade very sharp, with which she had to cut the rope at the moment when, by means of the string he held, he would pull the stool away from under Justine's feet.

'You see, girl,' he told her then, 'if you fail, I shan't. So I'm not wrong in saying that your life depends on you.'

The villain masturbated: it was at the moment of climax that he was to pull away the stool whose removal would leave Justine hanging from the roof. He did everything he could to fake this moment: if Justine happened to be clumsy, he would be delighted. But he waited in vain, she guessed in advance; the violence of his ecstasy betrayed him. Justine seized her opportunity; the stool slipped away, she cut the rope and fell to the ground, entirely free. There, unbelievably, although she was twelve feet away from the rascal, she was drenched in the jets of sperm that Roland emitted along with words of blasphemy.

Anyone other than Justine, no doubt, taking advantage of the weapon in her hands, would have at once hurled herself on this monster. How would this show of courage have helped her? Since she did not have the keys to those subterranean passages and was unacquainted with their detours, she would have died before she could have got out. Besides, Roland was on his guard. So she got up, leaving the weapon on the ground. Like that he would not have even the slightest suspicion about her. He had none; and, content with the meekness and the resignation of his victim, much more than with her skill, he signalled to her to go; and the two of them went back up to the château.

wickedness by introducing her to a society known as The Friends of Crime. Most of Juliette's adventures are long in the telling and difficult to present out of context, but one of them expresses the message Sade intends to convey. After she has been Saint-Fond's mistress for barely two years Juliette has amassed a fortune and likes to masturbate as she contemplates her jewels and her riches: she reaches orgasm as she thinks over this strange idea.

I love crime, and see all the means of crime at my disposal. O my friends, how sweet is this thought, and how much sexual juice has it made me lose! If I needed a new jewel, a new dress, my lover, who never wanted to see me more than three times in the same clothes, satisfied my wish immediately ... and he did all that without demanding more from me than disorder, frenzy, libertinage, and the most excessive care in the arrangements for his daily orgies. It was therefore by appeasing my tastes that all my tastes were in fact served; it was in giving myself over to every irregularity of my senses that my senses were intoxicated. But in what moral situation had so much ease placed me? That is what I dare not say, my friends, but I must all the same come to an agreement with you about it. The extreme debauchery in which I plunged myself every day had deadened the reactions of the soul, to such an extent that, assisted by the pernicious advice I received from all sides, I would not have deflected one sou of my riches in order to restore life to an unfortunate woman. About this time a terrible famine made itself felt in the neighbourhood of my property. All the inhabitants were reduced to the greatest distress. There were some terrible scenes: young girls enticed into a life of debauchery, children abandoned and several suicides. People came to implore my help. I remained firm, and very impertinently lent colour to my refusals by referring to the enormous expense that my gardens had demanded of me. Can one give money to charity, I asked with insolence, when one causes boudoirs made of mirrors to be built in the depths of one's arbours, and when one's walks are embellished with statues of Venus, Cupid and Sappho? In vain was everything most likely to touch me shown to my unmoved countenance. . . . Weeping mothers, naked children, spectres devoured by hunger; nothing disturbed me, nothing jolted my soul out of its normal state, and they obtained nothing from me but refusals. The result was that in taking stock of my sensations, I experienced, just as my teachers had instructed me, instead of the painful feeling a pity, a certain excitement, produced by the evil I believed I was doing in rejecting these unfortunates, which set coursing through my nerves a flame almost similar to that which burns in us every time we shatter some restraint or subjugate some prejudice. From that moment I realized how much pleasure could be gained from putting these principles into effect; and it was then that I perceived that just as the spectacle of misfortune, caused by fate, could provide a sensual pleasure for souls disposed or prepared by principles such as those which had been instilled in me, so the spectacle of misfortune, caused by oneself, must heighten this enjoyment. As you know, my intelligence always penetrates deeply into things, and you cannot imagine what possibilities and delights this aroused in me. The reasoning was simple: I experienced pleasure merely by refusing to put the unfortunate into a happy situation. What therefore would I not experience if I were myself the prime cause of this misfortune. If it is sweet to oppose good, I said to myself, it must be delicious to commit evil. I recalled and cherished this idea in those dangerous moments in which the body takes fire from the pleasures of the spirit. . . . Instants in which one denies oneself all the less because then nothing opposes the irregularity of one's wishes or the impetuosity of one's desires, and the resultant sensation is only violent in proportion to the multitude of restraints that have to be broken, or to their sacredness. Once the illusion had vanished, if one became moderate again, the inconvenience would be mediocre: it is the story of the sins of the mind. It is obvious that they offend nobody, but unfortunately one goes further. What would the realization of this idea be like, you venture to ask yourself, since its mere contact with my mind has moved me so deeply? You give life to the cursed illusion, and its existence is a crime.

A quarter of a league from my château there was a wretched cottage belonging to a very poor peasant named Martin-des-Granges, the father of eight children and the possessor of a wife who could be called a treasure for her wisdom and household management. Would you believe that this sanctuary of misfortune and virtue excited my rage and my depravity? It is true therefore that crime is a delectable thing: it is certain that the torch of lewdness is lit from the fire in which it consumes us . . . that crime alone awakens it within us and in order to make this delightful passion act as strongly as possible upon our nerves, only crime is needed.

Elvire and I had brought some Bologna phosphorus, and I had instructed this lively, witty girl to entertain the whole family while I placed it skilfully among the straw in an attic situated above the bedroom of these unfortunates. I returned and the children caressed me, while the mother told me with great good nature all the little details about her home. The father wished me to take some refreshment; zealously he offered me all the hospitality at his disposal. . . . None of that disarmed me, nothing softened me. I questioned myself, and far from that tedious feeling of pity I felt only a delightful tingling sensation throughout my entire body; the slightest touch would have given me an orgasm ten times over. I redoubled the caresses I was bestowing on each member of this interesting family, into whose bosom I came bringing murder; my treachery was at its peak; the more I betrayed, the greater my ecstasy. I gave ribbons to the mother, sweets to the children. We went back, but my delirium was such that I could not go home without begging Elvire to relieve the terrible state I was in. We hid ourselves in a thicket, I pulled up my skirts, I opened my thighs, she frigged me. . . . Barely had she touched me before I reached orgasm; I had never experienced such a terrible state of disorder. . . .

'What has madame done, then?'

'Horrors, atrocities, and the juices run deliciously when their flow gushes out from the midst of abomination. Frig me, Elvire, I must come.'

She slipped between my legs and sucked me.

'Oh, fuck,' I cried out to her, 'how right you are, you can see that I must resort to large-scale measures . . . you're using them. . . .'

And I flooded her lips. . . . We returned home, I was in a state that cannot be described, it seem to me that all disorders . . . all vices had simultaneously conspired together to debauch my heart; I experienced a sort of drunkenness . . . a sort of rage. . . . I was heartbroken at having touched only so small a portion of humanity. I should have liked the whole of nature to feel the distractions of my mind; I threw myself naked on the sofa in one of my boudoirs and ordered Elvire to bring me all my menservants, telling them they could do anything they liked with me, provided they insulted me and treated me like a tart. . . .'

[This they do, but one of the men says she ought to be taken not on a sofa but in the mud, and he drags her out to a heap of manure. Even two hours of this treatment do not 'satisfy the cruel state into which I was plunged by the idea of the crime I had just committed. When I returned to my boudoir we noticed the sky lit up. . . . Left alone with this beautiful girl I entreated her to go on frigging me'.]

'Let us go out . . .' I told her. 'I think I hear cries; let us go and savour this delightful spectacle . . . Elvire, it is my work, come and take your fill of it with me . . . I must see everything, I must hear everything, I want nothing to escape me.'

We went out . . . both of us with our hair loose, our dresses crumpled, we were intoxicated, we resembled bacchantes. Twenty paces from this scene of horror, behind a little mound that concealed us from the eyes of others, without preventing us from seeing everything, I fell once again into the arms of Elvire, herself almost as agitated as I was: we frigged each other by the light of the homicidal flames that my ferocity had lit . . . to the shrill cries of suffering and despair that my lust had occasioned, and I was the happiest of women.

[Despite her ecstasy Juliette is sad to discover, as she turns over the corpses with her foot, that two victims have escaped, the father and one of the children. However, like all Sade's homicidal characters, she has no difficulty in justifying her actions.]

'So that's what murder is, then! . . . A little disorganized matter, a few molecules shattered and flung back into the crucible of nature, who within a few days will give them back to the earth in a different form: what is the harm in that? Are a woman and a child more dear to nature than flies or worms? If I take away life from one of them I give it back to the other: so in what way am I doing wrong?'

[Juliette is proud to think that this is all her own work and her sexual disturbance is such that if she had been alone, she says, she might have been 'As cruel as the Caribbeans, I might perhaps have devoured my victims. . . .'

However, her conduct does not satisfy Lady Clairwil, one of her close friends.]

'There are three or four serious faults in the execution of this adventure,' she told me. 'Firstly' (and I am repeating all this to you so that you may better judge the character of this astonishing woman). 'Firstly,' she said, 'you were at fault in your behaviour, and if unfortunately anyone had come . . . from your disarray . . . from your gestures . . . you would have been judged guilty. Beware of this fault; as much ardour as you like inside, but on the surface, the utmost phlegm. When you can in this way restrain the effects of your lust, they will have more force.

'Secondly, your mind failed to see the thing on a large scale; for you will agree that when you have under your windows an immense city and seven or eight huge villages round about, there is a certain moderation . . . a certain modesty, in confining your frenzies to a single house, and that in a very isolated place . . . from fear that the flames, by spreading, might increase the extent of your little atrocity: I can see that you trembled when you committed it. And that therefore is an enjoyment spoilt, for those of crime will not permit restriction. I know them; if the imagination has not foreseen everything, if the hand has not accomplished everything, it is impossible for the delirium to be complete, because there will always remain a certain remorse . . . *I could have done more, and I did not*. And virtue's remorse is worse than that of crime: when you are accustomed to virtue and commit a bad deed, you always imagine that the host of good works will efface this stain, and since you can convince yourself easily of what you desire, you end up by calming yourself. But he who, like us, vigorously proceeds in the career of vice, never forgives himself a missed opportunity, because there is nothing to compensate him. Virtue does not come to his assistance; and the resolution that he makes to do something worse, by further exciting his mind with evil, will surely not console him for the chance to sin that he missed.

'Moreover, considering your plan only in outline,' continued Clairwil, 'there is still another great fault, for I would have followed up des Granges myself. In his position he could have been burnt as an incendiarist, and you will realize that if I had been in your place I should certainly not have missed that. When the house of an underling, as he was, on your estate, catches fire, are you not aware that you have the right to make inquiries through your justices whether or not he was guilty? How do you know that this man did not want to get rid of his wife and children in order to go and chase after women outside the district? As soon as he had shown you his back, you should have had him arrested as a fugitive, and handed him over to your justice as an incendiarist. With a few louis you would have found witnesses. Elvire herself would have done so. She would have testified that in the morning she saw this man roaming about in his attic, like a madman, that she questioned him and he could not answer her questions. And within a week they would have come and given you the voluptuous spectacle of seeing your man burnt at your own gate. May you profit from this lesson, Juliette, and never think of a crime without enlarging it; and while you are committing it, elaborate your ideas even more.'

'Such, my friends, were the cruel additions that Clairwil would have wished to see me make to the crime that I confessed to her, and I shall not conceal from you the fact that I was deeply affected by her reasoning, and promised myself faithfully never to fall into such grave errors again. The peasant's escape particularly grieved me, and I do not know what I would not have given to have seen him roasted at my gate. I have never consoled myself for this escape.'

[Justine's misadventures take place in France, but Juliette's most impressive achievements occur in Italy. She has fled there, after displeasing Saint-Fond through her momentary display of soft-heartedness. She had poisoned her own legal husband (she had married the elderly Comte de Lorsange for his money and soon dispatched him) and in Italy she quickly finds an escort, the villainous Sbrigani.

Sade knew the country well from his earlier visits, and added a footnote to the effect that his narrative was based on the true experiences of his former sister-in-law when she accompanied him there.

If Justine had always been used and abused by everyone she met, men and women, her sister Juliette, after the one early moment of weakness that drove her out of France, is perpetually in control of people and events. She is essentially preoccupied with power, money, sex and crime, all indissolubly linked. During her stay in Italy, which she describes with a strange mingling of reality and fantasy, she employs methods set out two centuries earlier by a famous native of the country, well known to Sade, Niccolò Machiavelli, whom he quoted in at least one footnote.

While in Italy Juliette becomes deeply involved in various lesbian relationships and also in arranging multiple deaths through poison. She had learnt the relevant secrets through a strange medium-like woman she had met earlier in France, Madame Durand.]

Everyone knows that the Italians make great use of poisons; their atrocious character is displayed through this method of serving their vengeance and their lewdness. With Sbrigani I had re-created all those for which la Durand had given me the receipts: I sold all kinds of them; an infinite number of people came to buy them from me and this branch of commerce earned me vast sums of money.

[One of her lovers asks her for a quick-acting poison to dispatch his mother. Juliette, scenting the opportunity for crime, tells the mother about his plans, the entire family were annihilated and the poison-maker insisted on sex with Sbrigani as she watched the funeral cortèges go past her window. Two daughters had been poisoned because for once Juliette had failed to seduce them.]

You can easily imagine, my friends, that in the midst of all these perfidious crimes, my personal lust was not forgotten. Since I had the power to choose among the superb men and sublime women whom I procured for others, you can well imagine that I began by taking those whom I found most pleasing: but the Italian men are not very potent and moreover their health, which is always suspect, drove me entirely into Sapphism. The Comtesse de Donis was at that time the most beautiful, the richest, the most elegant and the most lesbian woman in Florence. It was assumed in public that she was keeping me and this belief was not without some foundation.

Madame de Donis was a widow, thirty years old, as pretty as a picture, with a delightful appearance, much wit and many graces. I was attached to her through the bonds of libertinage and financial interest. We abandoned ourselves together to the most bizarre and the most unnatural excesses of shameless behaviour. I had taught the countess the art of stimulating her pleasures through all the refinements of cruelty, and the trollop, under my direction, was already almost as criminal; together we committed horrors.

[Juliette explains to her lover, with much Machiavellian detail, how to prepare and commit a crime, and especially how to desensitize oneself against any possible guilt. The countess admits that she had a crime in mind: she wishes to liquidate her mother and her daughter, Aglaé. The latter reminds her of her hated husband, whom she poisoned. She had another daughter, Fontange, agéd thirteen, whose father she adored, and wished to bequeath her fortune to her. Aglaé therefore must be removed. Juliette is bribed heavily so that she can assist in the crime and secretly plans to help herself to the countess's money. When the countess asks precisely how they would commit the murders Juliette explains:]

'Well,' I said, 'in the first place, the scene must be transported to the country. Only there are cruel acts of lust satisfactory. The silence and peace one enjoys there are found nowhere else. Then a few lewd details must be added to all that . . . is Aglaé a virgin?'

'Certainly.'

'Her virtue must be sacrificed on the altars of murder. Her two mothers must present her to the sacrificer, she must . . .'

'Ah! how terrifying are acts of torture!' interrupted the countess.

'No doubt, but let us not contrive them; let circumstances supply us with ideas for them. They will be infinitely more pleasurable.'

The rest of the night was taken up with the most refined acts of Sapphism. We kissed, we sucked, we devoured each other; armed as we both were with dildos, we inflicted the most formidable acts upon each other. And, having made all the arrangements for spending a few days in Prato, where the countess has a splendid house, we planned our delightful project for a week ahead.

Madame de Donis had very skilfully brought her mother and her daughter to the country place on the pretext of a six-month trip, during which she would allege that some illness had snatched away from her the victims whom her fury alone was to sacrifice. On my side I was to take along Sbrigani and two trusty valets on whom I could rely as surely as on myself. At Prato, therefore, on the appointed day, there were eight of us in all: my friend and myself, Sbrigani, the two valets, the mother, the daughter and an old duenna employed by Madame de Donis who had assisted her in all her disordered life for a long time.

I barely knew Aglaé; only now did I examine her much more closely. There was nothing in the world as pretty as this young person. Her figure was as pleasing as it was delicate, her skin incredibly white and fine, her big blue eyes always ready to light up, she had the most beautiful teeth, the most lovely hair. But all this was natural, without artifice. Aglaé was not inhabited by the graces, she was touched by them only lightly. You cannot imagine the impression this young woman made upon me; no woman had moved me so deeply for a long time.

An idea came into my head: let us change the victim, I said to myself, the trust which the countess has invested in me, is it not her own death warrant? If I truly wish to steal that money, as I do, should I not immediately terminate the life of the woman who entrusts it to me? I have come here to commit crimes. The one which ends the days of her daughter satisfies only my libertinage. The one which destroys the mother will at the same time inflame my passions and what is more will content my avarice.

[Juliette reflects that she will be rich, will have two pretty girls (i.e. Aglaé and Fontange) at her disposal, and will commit 'the refined murder of a woman whom I had caressed long enough not to want her any more'. The countess's old mother can easily be disposed of, but Juliette now wants Aglaé as her lover. Sbrigani approves of her plans and Juliette even arranges for all the servants, except the old duenna and her own two valets, to be sent away, while the countess's entire fortune must be brought to Prato, since it will be useful if anything goes wrong.]

The countess was so blinded on my account that nothing could open her eyes. . . . Madame de Donis agreed to everything; Aglaé was ordered to receive me in her bed, I took advantage of this the same evening. O my friends, what charms! Do not suspect me here of enthusiasm, or of metaphor, but in truth I do not exaggerate when I assure you that Aglaé could have served alone as a model for the man who did not find, even among the most beautiful women of Greece, enough beauty to compose from them the sublime

Venus that I had admired in the grand duke's* palace. Never, no never had I seen such delightful rounded shapes, such a voluptuous ensemble and details so absorbing; nothing as narrow as her pretty little cunt, nothing as plump as her delightful little bottom, nothing so well moulded as her breasts and I assure you now, speaking in cold blood,[†] that Aglaé was truly the most divine creature whom I had ever celebrated in my life. As soon as I discovered all these charms I devoured them with caresses, and moving rapidly from one attraction to another, I always felt as though I had not sufficiently caressed the one I had previously abandoned. The pretty little hussy, endowed with the lewdest of temperaments, soon fell into my arms. The roguish girl, who had been taught by her mother, caressed me like Sappho; but the skilful languors of my pleasures, my moments of anguish and tension, the exacerbation of my nerves, my spasms, my sighs, my blasphemies, all these attributes of studied corruption, all these signs of yielding and the deep arousal of nature, my words, my kisses, my touches, my lewd descriptions, everything astonished her, everything alarmed her sweet innocence and she finally admitted to me that my refinements left her mother far behind. Finally, after the most voluptuous hours, after we had both experienced orgasm in every possible way five or six times, after kissing each other and sucking every part of our bodies, after having bitten, pinched, licked and whipped each other, after having, in a word, done everything that could be invented in the way of the foulest, the dirtiest, the most exaggerated, the most inconceivable things, I spoke to this delightful creature in more or less the following terms:

'Dear girl,' I said to her, 'I don't know what principles you possess, and if the countess, in giving you the first lessons

---

* The grand duke was Leopold II of Tuscany.
† Juliette was still recounting her life story.

in pleasure, has paid attention to the cultivation of your mind. But whatever the situation, what I have to reveal to you is too important for me to conceal it from you for one moment. Your mother, the most false, the most dishonourable, the most criminal of women, has conspired against your life: tomorrow you are due to be her victim, if you don't ward off the blow by striking it first. . . .'

'So that is the cause of the coldness she has been showing me for some time, of her treatment . . .'

'What treatment have you received from her, then?'

Aglaé confessed to me that her mother, who had become cruel in pleasure, had been tormenting her, smacking her, beating her and saying the harshest things to her. Since I was curious to know how far la Donis had taken disorder and aberration in the pleasures she had allowed herself with her daughter, I discovered that she had demanded from this girl one of the lewd deviations of which the violence hastens disgust. This shameless mother, open to all possible kinds of libertinage, practised only one form of enjoyment with her daughter now, that of making her shit in her mouth and swallowing the result.

'Dear love,' I said to this young person, 'you should have shown more restraint in the favours you granted your mother. Too much compliance has produced satiation. There is no longer any time, the moment has come, it is only a question of informing her.'

[Juliette soon persuaded Aglaé to commit the crime of matricide and rejoiced in her success, deeply entertained by her own treason. She made love to the girl again and to her delight 'I made her experience orgasm at the idea of assassinating her mother. We got up.'

The crime is to be committed in the drawing-room, following the countess's own plan.]

. . . but instead of being the agent, the wretched woman was the victim. Her daughter and I lay in a baignoire, caressing each other. Sbrigani sprinkled us with the blood of the two mothers; he made it spurt from endless different wounds. At this juncture I can say that to the honour of Aglaé her courage and resolution did not weaken for a moment; moving easily from pleasure to ecstasy the end of the operation was the sole limit of her delirium, and the scene was long. It is impossible to describe the refinements that Sbrigani invented in order to prolong the tortures; the monster concluded them by sodomizing his victims: they expired beneath him.

[The incident does not end there. Sbrigani, less ruthless in some ways than Juliette, even feels some remorse at what he has done: '". . . only the rape of this girl can console me for the murder of the two mothers: hand her over to me, Juliette". And, barely waiting for my reply the libertine, who was in a state of powerful erection, seized the girl and took her virginity. Her thighs were barely tinged with the blood emerging from this young cunt before the Italian reversed the coin and with three twists of his body he was in her arse'.

After a series of unimaginable cruelties inflicted on Aglaé Juliette and Sbrigani half dig up the corpses of the countess and her mother and half bury Aglaé nearby so that she can die facing them. The old duenna is shot, Juliette and Sbrigani collect the countess's riches and with their two trusted servants leave for Rome. Once there Juliette immediately becomes the lover of Princess Olympe de Borghese and soon encounters the Pope. The Princess Olympe de Borghese made an immediate approach to Juliette, inviting her to supper 'in her small country house near Rome'.]

'We shall be alone,' she told me, 'you seem to me a delightful woman, my dear countess, and I want absolutely to have a relationship with you.'

You can easily judge that following such advances all ceremony was soon banished. It was excessively hot. After a supper, as voluptuous as it was copious, served to us by five charming girls in a small arbour-room of roses and jasmine, surrounded by waterfalls, their pleasant murmur and sweet coolness uniting all the charms of nature and the attractions of art, the princess, her way lit by her nymphs, took me to a small isolated pavilion standing beneath shady poplar trees. We entered a circular room, around which there was a circular sofa, no more than eight inches high and entirely strewn with cushions; mirrors, multiplied to an infinite extent, supplied the finishing touch which made this small place into one of the loveliest temples of Venus in Italy. The young girls lit a few lamps filled with scented oil, while their flames, concealed behind green gauze, could not offend the eyes, then they withdrew.

[The two women immediately decide to call each other by their Christian names, especially since Olympe does not wish to be reminded of 'the bonds of marriage'. They kiss.]

'Dear Olympe,' I said, seizing this enchanting creature in my arms, 'what would I not agree to with you? Has not nature, in endowing you with so many charms, granted you rights over all hearts, and are you not certain of seducing all those creatures who will be consumed by your eyes?'

'You are divine, my dear Juliette, kiss me a thousand, thousand times!' replied Olympe, subsiding on to the ottoman. . . . 'O my most affectionate friend, I feel that we are going to do so many things together. . . . But I'm afraid of telling you everything, I'm so libertine, make no mistake about it, dear heart, I adore you; but it isn't love that inflames me for you now: I don't know love without lust, I adopt only its lewdness.'

'O heavens!' I cried, 'is it possible that, born five hundred leagues apart from each other, nature has formed two souls so much alike!'

'What, Juliette,' Olympe replied swiftly, 'are you a libertine as well? We shall caress each other without loving, we shall experience orgasm like trollops, without shame, without delicacy, we shall include other people in our pleasures! Ah, let me devour you, my angel, let me kiss you a thousand, thousand times! It's satiation that leads us here . . . it's habit, it's the extreme opulence in which we both live. We're accustomed to refuse ourselves nothing, we're satiated with everything, and stupid people don't understand where this apathy of the soul can lead us.'

Olympe, as she talked, undressed me, undressed herself and, both of us naked, we were soon in each other's arms. Borghese's first gestures were to fall at my knees, open my thighs, place both hands on my buttocks and thrust her tongue as far as it would go into my arse. I was in such a state of intoxication that the tribad quickly triumphed, she swallowed my juices. I threw her down, and, pulling both of us on to the cushions strewn over the boudoir, I lay down in reverse on top of her, my head was between her legs and I sucked her with all my strength, the roguish woman performed the same service for me. In this way we reached orgasm five or six times.

'We are not enough for each other,' Olympe told me. 'It's impossible for two women alone to find satisfaction: let's bring in the girls who waited on us. They're beautiful, the eldest is not yet seventeen, the youngest is fourteen. No days go by without their caressing me. Would you like to have them?'

'Oh, certainly, I like all that sort of thing, as you do. Anything that increases libertinage is precious to my senses.'

'One cannot multiply its effects too much,' replied Olympe wildly, 'nothing is so tedious as those timid, reserved or squeamish women who never experience any pleasure outside love and stupidly imagine that in order to fuck you must adore each other.'

And since the princess had rung, the five young girls, aware of this little lustful arrangement, came to us totally naked. Nothing was as pretty as their faces, nothing as fresh and well shaped as their bodies, and as they surrounded Olympe I felt for a moment that I was watching the Graces encircling Venus.

'Juliette,' the princess said to me, 'I'm going to sit facing you. The five girls will surround you, and through the most amorous titillations, the most lascivious postures, they will make you achieve orgasm. I shall watch it happen, that's all I want. You can't imagine the pleasure I experience on seeing a pretty woman in a state of ecstasy. During that time I shall masturbate, I'll let my imagination range free. I assure you it will travel far.'

The proposal appealed too much to my lust for me to refuse it. Olympe arranged the groups. One of these pretty girls, crouching over me, had me sucking a pretty little cunt; I myself was suspended on a kind of harness composed of padded webbing covered in black satin and my buttocks touched the face of a second girl who licked my arse-hole; the third girl, stretched out over me, licked my cunt and I caressed the clitoris of each of them with one hand. Olympe, who was devouring this spectacle as she watched, held in her hand a silken cord which controlled the harness on which I was suspended, and as she pulled gently on this cord she bestowed on me a forward and backward movement which prolonged and multiplied the tongue action which I was giving and receiving, and by the delectable motion it produced, brought about an unbelievable increase in pleasure. I do not think I had ever relished such joy. I had been unaware until then of the enhanced delight that Olympe was preparing for me when the delicious sound of music was heard, without its source being discernible. Living out the visions of the Koran, I believed I had been transported into its paradise and there, surrounded by the houris that it promised to the faithful, I thought they were caressing me only to plunge me into the deepest excesses of the most delectable lust. The movements transferred to me by Olympe took place now only in time to the music; I was in heaven, I existed now only through the profound awareness of my lust. After an hour of intoxication Olympe came into the swing, surrounded like me by the five girls. Enjoyably touched by the music which intoxicated us with its constantly varied tender melodies, I made love to her for an hour and more in this pleasure machine; then, a moment of rest having followed, we varied our pleasures.

[The new delights consisted in further group sex with the girls.]

The music continued; Olympe asked me if I would like the musicians brought in.

'I agree to it,' I replied. 'I should like to be seen by the entire universe, in my present state of intoxication.'

Olympe then expresses the same belief in sexual anarchy as does Dolmancé in *La Philosophie dans le Boudoir*: all women should behave like prostitutes. 'How imbecile are those who do not sacrifice everything to their pleasures: ah, how stupid are those who can have any other gods except Venus . . . any other type of behaviour than that of prostituting themselves continually to all sexes, to all ages, to all living creatures.'

[Olympe is carried away by her convictions.]

'I feel I am on the brink of hurling myself into horrifying debauchery; all prejudices fade before my eyes, all restrictions yield before me; I decide on the greatest deviations, the bandage falls from my eyes: I see the abyss and I leap into it with delight. I trample underfoot that imaginary honour in which women stupidly destroy their happiness, without receiving any compensation for the sacrifices made. Honour lies in opinion, but the opinion which brings happiness is one's own, not that of others. If we are sensible enough to despise that public opinion, which leads us to happiness only through privations, then we shall soon realize that it is possible to live just as happily, after becoming the object of universal disdain, as beneath the sorrowful wreaths of honour.'

[Juliette, as she listens, finds Olympe as 'beautiful as the day in this moment of effervescence', but she wants her friend to go further: 'No, no, dear Olympe, no, you do not yet know where crimes of lust can lead.' Olympe reminds her friend that she poisoned her first husband and the same fate awaits her second. That is still not enough for Juliette: '. . . the crime already committed, the crime that is planned, these are necessary crimes, and those I demand from you are gratuitous, unnecessary crimes'.

Her phrase, *des crimes gratuits*, anticipates the doctrine of *l'acte gratuit*, the gratuitous acts and crimes discussed or described by later writers, including Lautréamont, Gide, Camus.

Olympe is convinced: 'She understood me marvellously well, her mind was disordered and the wretch swore to me that we should not separate until we had perpetrated together some of these voluptuous horrors.'

First, however, there are other pleasures.]

And just when she [Olympe] was in a state of prodigious agitation the musicians appeared. Ten young men aged between sixteen and twenty made up the consort. Nothing could have looked more attractive; they were clad in thin gauze, in the Greek manner. At a mere sign from Olympe they were naked.

[She then indulges in complicated sex with the group, and asks for Juliette's approval. 'Yes, no doubt, I'm fairly pleased, but one can do better, and I'll convince you of it.']

The young girls were at once ordered by me to bring the young men into a state of erection again. As soon as their penises were up in the air I gave myself to them. They were supple . . . agile . . . I put two in my cunt, one in my bottom, I sucked one, two were placed under my armpits, one in my hair, I caressed one with each hand, the tenth masturbated over my eyes: but I forbade emission. They were all to go through ten variations; all of them, in turn, were to sacrifice at each of the temples offered to their lust: the dénouement was permitted only after that. The handsome boys, singularly aroused by these preludes, flooded me with sperm, and la Borghese, who, while being caressed by her young girls, had examined me with extreme pleasure, agreed that my execution was more skilful than hers.

[The two women then arrange sexual interplay for the young men and women and join in themselves. Juliette is pleased when Olympe begins to show orgasmic pleasure at the sight of pain inflicted on others.

Eventually it is time for a rest.]

Olympe, exhausted, spoke of going to table. We passed into a room as delightfully furnished as it was magnificently illuminated. Without any orders being given, a superb collation was served in a large basket of flowers which seemed to have been thrown into a huge orange tree laden with fruit; I wanted to eat one of these fruits, they were made of ice. All the rest was equally surprising, everything revealed the most sensitive taste and the most sumptuous elegance. The girls alone served us; the young men, who had withdrawn behind the décor, delighted us now only with the sound of their melodious instruments.

[Olympe and Juliette, both intoxicated with lust, are soon equally so with wine and liqueurs.]

'Now,' I said to my companion, 'let us terminate things with some vile deed.'

'Command. I'm ready for everything.'

'Let us sacrifice one of these girls.'

'This one,' said Olympe, presenting me the prettiest of the five.

'What! you agree?'

'And why shouldn't I imitate you? Do you think that murder frightens me? . . . Ah! you'll see if I'm worthy of being your student.'

[The two women realize they have no instruments of torture available. However, they spend a couple of hours burning the girl with candles. Juliette suggests hanging her up by the nipples. For two more hours they stick pins into her until she dies. The women then sleep for five hours and finally bury the corpse under a clump of trees. They separate, 'both protesting that we would not stop there, after making such a good start'.

These sexual frenzies, however, become so repetitive as to be ridiculous, whereas Juliette's discussions with the Pope about religion and the Church are fascinating, even if the reader knows her (Sadean) views in advance. He admires her intelligence and strength of mind but is alarmed at the conditions she sets before she will consent to sexual intercourse with him. One of them entails the celebration of a black mass in St Peter's with the massacre of many young people. The Pope carries out Juliette's wishes.

Juliette meets many larger-than-life characters such as Brisa-Testa, who lives incestuously with his sister, her old friend Lady Clairwil. Juliette listens to the story of his life, which forms a novel within the novel. Then there is Minski, the Russian giant who eats only human flesh, and offers it to his guests. He too was said to be based on a legendary character from earlier times. And Brisa-Testa, while on a visit to Russia, had encountered Catherine the Great.

Her life in Italy makes Juliette conceive crimes on an ever larger scale. She and Clairwil, tired of Olympe de Borghese, eventually throw her into the flames of Vesuvius and arrange to burn down the hospices in Rome, thereby killing a great number of poor orphan girls. All these achievements afford Juliette great satisfaction. Since murder within the family was not considered any more of a crime than any other killing, Juliette also dispatches her own daughter.

When he reached the last few pages of his story Sade presumably aimed to show that only Juliette, prosperous in her vice, deserved approval, whereas Justine was doomed to failure and suffering, even in death. Juliette decides that the tediously prudish Justine must be turned out of the house at once, without any money. A thunderstorm is imminent. The girl is struck by lightning and when the libertine company undress her corpse they find that 'the lightning, which had entered through her mouth, had emerged through her vagina'. Juliette and her friends then exult, and following the example of an abbé who is present, the men indulge in sex with the dead body and Juliette masturbates with delight as she watches them.

In one way Sade had reached the end of the road: when he had first drafted the story of the two sisters, presumably in the early 1780s, Juliette, after the death of Justine, had retired to a convent and lived her last years as a model of virtue. Now, in 1797, all was changed: Juliette lives for ten more successful years and dies a normal death.]

... and this woman, unique of her kind, who died without having written the last events of her life, removed from all writers the possibility of revealing it to the public. Those who would wish to undertake it would only do so by offering us their dreams as realities, which would look very different to the eyes of people with taste, and particularly to those who have taken some interest in the reading of this work.

If Juliette is a *maîtresse-femme*, an early and repulsive representation of fantasy-feminism, she is not entirely self-reliant. She cannot manage without Sbrigani, even if she needs only his biceps and his penis. She is certainly the brains of the ménage. She is the most extreme of all Sade's characters, more studied that any of his crude and villainous men. An analysis of the contrasts between Juliette and Justine, for which there is no space here, provides one of the possible keys to the long-lasting, perhaps insolvable enigma of Sade.

No woman can read *Justine* without a shudder. Could these horrors happen to *me*? she asks. Unlikely – for most of them belong to the world of fantasy and surely nobody possesses the girl's capacity for survival. But the story is a warning.

Yet the same woman might read *Juliette* with some confusion. Could *I* achieve the necessary power over myself and others to commit crimes of this atrocious magnitude? Unlikely again; but if, as with the sufferings of Justine, they belong to the world of fantasy, they occurred within the mind of at least one man.

No wonder Simone de Beauvoir said of Sade: '. . . the supreme value of his testimony is that it disturbs us'.

Sade later denied authorship of the book, saying he had been merely the copyist. Along with *La Nouvelle Justine* it seems to have sold well, in secret, until Bonaparte, having appointed himself First Consul in 1799, ordered that the bookshops should be cleaned up.

# La Philosophie dans le Boudoir

## ou Les Instituteurs Immoraux

Six years, 1791–7, had passed between the publication of the second and third versions of *Justine*, plus *L'Histoire de Juliette*, as far as the dates and the numbers of these clandestine versions can be ascertained. It had taken another six years, 1789–95, to complete and publish, this time openly, *Aline et Valcour*. These years of turmoil, which had brought the execution of King Louis XVI, the Convention, the Terror and the Directory, had brought also many adventures for Sade. His freedom in 1790 had not gained him a quiet life, no doubt because he was incapable of such an existence. Despite calling himself Citizen Sade, despite his appointment to the Section des Piques (forty-eight of these administrative divisions had been set up), despite his publication of various stirring democratic pamphlets, he incurred danger through administrative mistakes and his hard to deny aristocratic past.

His name had wrongly been included on a list of émigrés, which could have ended his life, and he was accused of royalist sympathies. During 1793 and 1794 he found himself in three prisons, converted convents where conditions were appalling. He was even condemned to death at one point, but through vigorous self-defence, good luck and the volatile moods of the time, he was freed in the summer of 1794. He had also been responsible for the freedom of others: through the power he possessed in the Section des Piques (he had become president at one stage) he could, if he had so wished, have sent his former parents-in-law, the Président de Montreuil and his vindictive wife, to their deaths. He spared them: did he not wish to take his revenge on madame? In reality, no, he had already done so in the fantasy world of his writings.

If he himself had survived threats to his liberty and his life, he did not escape poverty. He was struggling to support himself, to help Marie-Constance and her son and to find some way of repaying his separated wife's dowry. The Château de La Coste had been vandalized in 1792, but eventually Sade was lucky enough to sell it some four years later. Money was still needed, desperately so, and he made another hopeful attempt to earn it by the only method he knew, by writing. If income from writing was unreliable he was still more hopeful of earning more from it than he received from his lawyer in Provence, despite all his desperate pleas.

Sade now planned a short book with a tempting theme which could only be described as pornographic: the initiation of an innocent girl into the mysteries of sex, all its mysteries, including perversions and the complete repertoire of libertinage. He may have written some of it earlier, in an attempt to reconstitute *Les Cent Vingt Journées de Sodome*, which he believed lost. In any case, he worked hard in grim conditions. It was so cold during the winter in which he was writing that the ink froze in his ink-well and there was no wood for heating.

*La Philosophie dans le Boudoir* appeared anonymously in 1795. The author had decided to refer to it as a 'posthumous book by the author of Justine', and the title-page describes it as published 'in London', a useful lie. The work consists of seven dialogues with a few stage directions. Eugénie, a girl of fifteen whose very name seems to have been chosen with care, is welcomed to the boudoir, that useful place situated between the salon and the bedroom, by Madame de Saint-Ange, named surely with sardonic humour, for no woman could have had less in common with saints or angels. She is to be helped in the initiation by her brother, the Chevalier de Mirvel, and more particularly by the middle-aged libertine Dolmancé.

[Eugénie learns with rapidity about the male anatomy, the existence of the cock and its attendant balls (the more correct term, she is told, is testicles). The lessons she receives are only half concerned with straightforward, heterosexual sex, for Dolmancé is interested solely in anal penetration, while Madame de Saint-Ange explains that it is less painful than any other, and much safer, for it prevents the danger of pregnancy. When Eugénie asks why there are so many mirrors in this boudoir her teacher explains.]

'It is because they repeat attitudes in a thousand different ways, they multiply to an infinite extent the same delights in the eyes of those who are relishing them on this ottoman. By this means no part of either body can be hidden: everything must be on view; this method assembles just as many groups round those in the grip of love, just as many imitators of their pleasures, just as many delectable tableaux which inflame their lust and soon bring it to a conclusion.'

[Madame de Saint-Ange actually uses the word *amour*, usually the missing ingredient in all the sexual postures described by Sade in such infinitely detailed and always monotonous physiological terms. The whole of this short book would seem to deny the existence of any feelings outside lust and self-indulgence, but paradoxically Sade now decided, as he had done in *Juliette*, in fact to explain, as part of his 'philosophy', what love is and how it is to be avoided at all costs. It is Dolmancé who is chosen to set out its many disadvantages.]

'You speak to me about the bonds of love, Eugénie. May you never experience them! Ah! may such a sentiment, in view of the happiness I wish you, never come close to your heart! What is love? One may consider it, I think, only as the effect a beautiful object exerts over us; these effects carry us away; they inflame us; if we possess this object then we are content; if it is impossible to possess it, we are in despair. But what is the basis of that sentiment? . . . desire. What are the consequences of that sentiment? . . . madness. Let us therefore cling to the motive, and guarantee for ourselves its effects. The motive is to possess the object: well then, let us try to succeed, but carefully so; let us enjoy it as soon as we possess it; if we cannot do so, let us console ourselves: a thousand other similar objects, and often much better ones, will console us for the loss of that one; all men, all women feel the same: no love resists calm reflection. Oh! how deceptive is that intoxication which absorbs in us the effects of the senses, puts us in such a state that we no longer see, we no longer exist except through that madly adored object! But can that be called living? Is it not rather depriving us voluntarily of all the pleasures of life? Is it not wishing to remain in a burning fever which absorbs us and devours us, without leaving us any happiness beyond metaphysical enjoyments, so similar to the effects of madness? If we should still love this adorable object, if it were certain that we should never relinquish it, this would no doubt still be extravagant behaviour, but at least it would be excusable. Does that happen? Have we many examples of those eternal relationships which are never renounced? A few months of enjoyment, soon returning the object to its true place, make us blush at the thought of the incense we burnt on its altars, and we often reach the point when we cannot even imagine that it could have seduced us to this point.

'O girls who love pleasure, let us have your bodies as

much as you can! Fuck, amuse yourselves, that is the essential; but avoid love with care. The physical side is the only good thing about it, said the naturalist Buffon. . . .'

[Sade reiterated the plea he so often made, that women should be vulvivagous, polygamous. They must not allow one man to captivate them,]

. . . for the purpose of this constant love, as it linked him to you, would be to prevent you from giving yourself to another, a cruel form of selfishness which would soon be fatal to your pleasures. Women are not made for one man: nature created them for everyone. Let them hear only this sacred voice and give themselves indiscriminately to everyone who wants them. Always trollops, never lovers, fleeing love, adoring pleasure, they will find only roses in the path of life; they will bestow on us only flowers!

Love: Sade knew what it was, he had experienced it when young, with the girl he had wanted to marry, with la Beauvoisin, with his sister-in-law. But if he had received any response, it had been short-lived; and even his loveless, if useful marriage had come to an end. He had the devoted affection of Marie-Constance, whom he called 'Sensible' (Sensitive), but how far had lack of love, love given and love received, been the cause of all his destructive behaviour in early life, soon taken to wild excess in the fantasies of his writing? We shall never know.

The 'philosophers' in the boudoir are fantasists too, despite their object-lessons in physiology. As soon as Madame de Saint-Ange announces that she has had twelve thousand lovers in twelve years of marriage, the reader does not accept her teaching very seriously. In some ways Sade had worked out his seven dialogues neatly, for Eugénie's education is to be completed by two men, each one appreciating two different aspects of the female body, in crude terms the cunt and the bottom, and he manoeuvres the quartet of people into a sexual architecture like a team of acrobats. For most of the book he avoids cruelty and there are even moments of humour. When the exhausted teachers co-opt Augustin, a lusty eighteen-year-old gardener, to help them, Eugénie, having just lost her virginity to the chevalier, protests that the young man's enormous member will kill her.

'Oh no, mam'selle,' replies Augustin, 'nobody has ever died from it.'

The way the scene continues is typical of the book.

DOLMANCÉ: One moment, my fine son, one moment: she has to present me her bottom while you do the fucking. . . . Yes, so, Madame de Saint-Ange, come closer: I promised to penetrate you, I'll keep my word; but place yourself so that while fucking you I shall be in a position to whip Eugénie. At the same time the chevalier must whip me. (*All the arrangements are made.*)

[Eugénie does not seem to suffer and is now so corrupt that she says 'in this intoxicated state I would go if I had to and have myself fucked in the streets!']

DOLMANCÉ: How beautiful she looks!
EUGÉNIE: I hate you, you rejected me!
DOLMANCÉ: Could I go against my dogmatic beliefs?
EUGÉNIE: Very well, then, I forgive you, and I should respect principles which lead to my disorders. How could I not adopt them, I who wish now to live only a criminal life?'

At this point in the Fifth Dialogue Sade, as though suddenly bored with physiology, had Dolmancé produce a brochure he has just bought at the Palais de l'Egalité. Eugénie, feeling in need of a rest, has asked a crucial question: 'I should like to know if morals are really necessary in a government, if their influence counts in the spirit of a nation.'

Since the chevalier has a fine voice he is chosen to read the brochure, long enough to be more tiring than any session of group sex. Sade may well have written this piece earlier and now found a means of publishing it. *Français, encore un effort*: the phrase has become as famous as any by Rousseau or Tom Paine. 'Frenchmen, yet one more effort, if you wish to be republicans. . . .' And then, with his uniquely illogical logic, Sade proved that religion must be abolished. Then comes the turn of morality.]

At all times a man's duties have been considered in three different groups as follows:

1. Those dictated by his conscience and credulity in relation to the Supreme Being.
2. Those that he is obliged to fulfil in relation to his fellow-men.
3. Finally those that relate only to himself.

We should now be certain that there is no god with any interest in us, and that we are creations made necessary by nature, like plants and animals, being in this world because it was impossible for us not to be in it. This certainty undoubtedly destroys with one blow, as can be seen, the first part of these duties, those, I mean, for which we falsely hold ourselves responsible to the Deity. All religious transgressions vanish with them, all those known by vague and indeterminate names such as *impiety*, *sacrilege*, *blasphemy*, *atheism*, etc., all those in fact for which Athens punished so unjustly *Alcibiades*, and France the unfortunate *La Barre*. . . .*

Let us now turn to the second class of man's duties, those binding him to his fellows. This class is the most extensive of all.

* The Chevalier de La Barre was decapitated and burnt for alleged sacrilege in 1766, aged nineteen.

Christian morality, which is too vague about man's relationship with his fellow-men, lays down foundations so full of sophistries that we cannot possibly admit them, because if you wish to construct principles you must avoid basing them on sophistries. This . . . morality tells us indeed to love our neighbour as ourselves. Certainly nothing would be more sublime – if something which is false can ever possess the characteristics of beauty. There is no question of loving our fellows as ourselves because that is against the law of nature, and our whole lives must be directed only by her agency. It is only necessary to love our neighbours like brothers, like friends given to us by nature, and with whom we should live all the better in a republican state because the disappearance of distinctions must necessarily strengthen our ties.

Henceforth let humanity, fraternity and benevolence prescribe for us our reciprocal duties, according to these principles, and let us fulfil them each with the simple degree of energy that nature granted us for that purpose without blaming, and above all without punishing, those colder, more splenetic characters who do not find in these ties, touching though they are, all the sweet rewards experienced by others. For it will be agreed that it would be a palpable absurdity in this case to wish to lay down universal laws. Such a procedure would be as ridiculous as if the general of an army wished to dress all his soldiers in uniforms of the same size. It is a terrible injustice to expect men, whose temperaments are unequal, to bind themselves to identical laws; what suits one does not suit another.

I recognize that it is impossible to make as many laws as there are men, but the laws could be so easy and so small in number that all men, whatever their natures, could easily submit to them. I would further demand that this small number of laws be of the kind that is easily adaptable to every different character, the guiding principle being to strike in varying degrees, according to the individual to be affected. It is clear that the practice of particular virtues is impossible for certain men, as there are particular remedies which do not suit certain temperaments. Would it not, therefore, be the height of injustice for you to bring down the law upon a man incapable of submitting to it?

Would not the iniquity you would thereby commit be as great as that of which you would be guilty if you tried to force a blind man to distinguish colours?

It follows from these first principles, one feels, that it is necessary to make the law mild and above all to eliminate for ever the atrocity of the death penalty, because the law is by its very nature cold and cannot be moved by passions which in a man may justify the cruel act of murder. Man receives impulses from nature which enable him to pardon this act, but the law on the other hand is always in opposition to nature and receives nothing from her. It has no authority to permit itself the same motives, and cannot possibly have the same rights. These are learned and subtle distinctions which escape many people because very few people think, but they will be welcomed by the educated audience I am addressing, and will have an influence, I hope, upon the new Code that is in preparation.

The second reason for abolishing the death penalty is that it has never stamped out crime, which goes on every day at the very foot of the gallows.

This punishment must be removed in fact, because there is no worse calculation than to kill a man for having killed another. The obvious result of this procedure is that where before there was one man less, suddenly there are two less, and only executioners and imbeciles can be familiar with such arithmetic.

Be that as it may, the sins that we can commit against our brothers can be reduced in the end to four main groups; *calumny*, *theft*, offences proceeding from *impurity* which can disagreeably affect others, and *murder*.

All these actions were considered capital offences in a monarchical regime; are they so serious in a republican state? We shall analyse this question in the light of philosophy, for only in this way should such an examination be conducted. Do not accuse me of being a dangerous innovator, or tell me that there is a risk of softening the action of remorse on the conscience of the wrongdoer, as may perhaps be caused by these words, that it would be overwhelmingly wrong to increase the tendency to crime in the heart of the same wrongdoer by the mildness of my morality. I formally testify here that I have no such perverse intentions. I am expounding ideas which have crystallized within me since the age of reason, ideas whose flow, for so many centuries, has been opposed by the infamous despotism of tyrants; so much the worse for those who would be corrupted by these great ideas, so much the worse for those who can fasten upon the evil only in philosophical views, which are capable of being corrupted to any need. Who knows if these people would not perhaps be poisoned by reading Seneca and Charron? It is not to them that I speak; I speak only to those capable of understanding me, and they will read me without danger.

I confess with the utmost frankness that I have never believed calumny to be wrong, especially in a constitution like ours where all men are closer to each other, more intimately linked, and obviously have a greater interest in knowing one another better. There are two possibilities: calumny is either directed against a truly wicked man or it lights upon a man of virtue. It will be agreed that in the first case it makes hardly any difference if a little more evil is spoken about a man already known for his many sins. It may even happen then that the non-existent evil will throw a little light upon that which does exist, and then will the evildoer be better known.

Imagine there is an unhealthy influence in Hanover, but

that in exposing myself to this inclement air the only risk I run is catching a bout of fever. Would I have any grievance against a man who told me, in order to stop my going, that a visit there would kill me? No, without a doubt, for by frightening me with a major evil, he has prevented me from suffering a minor one.

What, on the other hand, when calumny strikes the virtuous man? There is nothing to be alarmed about, let him show himself and all the venom of the slanderer will soon rebound upon himself. For such people calumny is but a purifying test from which their virtue will emerge only more radiant. There is even some profit in this for the total sum of virtues in a republic, because the sensitive and virtuous man, stung by the injustice he has just experienced, will devote himself to even better efforts. He will wish to triumph over this calumny from which he thought he was protected, and his good actions will acquire only a further degree of strength. Thus, in the first case the slanderer will have produced good enough results in exaggerating the vices of the dangerous man, and in the second he will have produced excellent results in forcing virtue to display itself in its entirety.

Therefore I ask you now in what respect you can have anything to fear from a calumniator, especially in a state where it is essential to distinguish the wicked and to increase the power to the good? So beware then of pronouncing any penalty against calumny, and regard it in two ways, as a warning light and as a stimulant, and in any case as something very useful. The legislator whose ideas must all be of the same magnitude as the work on which he is engaged, must never study the effect of crime in its individual aspect only. It is the mass effect that must be examined, and when he observes the effects resulting from calumny in this light, I defy him to find in them anything to punish; I defy him to be able to attach any shadow of justice to the law that punishes it. On the other hand he will be the most just and upright of men if he favours and rewards it.

Theft is the second of the moral wrongs we propose to scrutinize.

If we scan the records of antiquity we shall see that theft was allowed, rewarded, in all the republics of Greece. Sparta and Lacedaemonia openly favoured it; several other nations regarded it as a soldierly virtue. It is certain that it fosters courage, strength, dexterity, all the virtues in fact useful to a republican constitution, and consequently to our own. I would dare to ask, without partiality now, whether theft, the effect of which is to equalize wealth, is a great evil in a state whose aim is equality? Surely not, for if it maintains equality on one side, it makes the other side more scrupulous in preserving its wealth. There was one nation that punished not the thief but him who let himself be robbed, in order to teach him to look after his property. This leads us to a wider field of reflection.

God forbid that I wish here to attack or destroy the oath of respect for property lately taken by the nation; but may I be allowed a few ideas on the injustice of this oath? What is the essence of an oath sworn by all the individuals of a nation? Is it not the maintenance of perfect equality between citizens, the equal submission of all to the law protecting the property of all? And therefore I now ask if a law is very just that orders the man with nothing to respect the man with everything? What are the elements of the social pact? Do they not consist in the surrender of a small part of your liberty and property in order to preserve and safeguard what you retain of both?

All laws rest on these foundations; they are the motives for the punishments inflicted on the man who abuses his freedom. In the same way they authorize taxation. The reason why a citizen does not cry out against the demands made upon him is that what he gives is the means for safeguarding what remains to him. But, once again, by what right shall the man with nothing bind himself to a contract that protects only the man with everything? If you are performing an act of equity in defending the property of the rich with your oath, are you not doing an injustice in extracting this oath from a defender who has nothing? What interest is there for the latter in your oath? Why do you want him to promise something in favour only of the man who differs from him so much by his riches? Surely there is nothing more unjust: an oath should have an equal effect on all who take it. It is impossible for it to bind a man with no interest in keeping it, for then it would no longer be the agreement of a free people; it would be the weapon of the strong against the weak, and against that the latter should rebel unceasingly. Now that is what happens in the oath of respect for property that the nation has just demanded; the rich alone bind the poor with it, and the rich alone have an interest in this oath, which the poor swear without reflecting that this vow, extorted from their good faith, is the means of engaging them to do something that cannot be done on their behalf. Convinced then as you must be of this barbarous inequality, do not aggravate your injustice by punishing him who has nothing for daring to steal something from him who has everything. Your inequitable oath gives him more right to this than ever. In making him perjure himself with this oath, which for him is so absurd, you justify every crime to which this perjury may lend him. You no longer have the right to punish that of which you were the cause. I need say no more to make you realize the horrible cruelty of punishing thieves. Emulate the wise law of the nation I have just mentioned; punish the man so negligent as to let himself be robbed, but do not threaten punishment against the robber. Realize that your oath has authorized this action for him, and that in giving in to it he is only following the first and most sacred impulse of nature, self-preservation at no matter whose expense.

We shall now examine in this second class of man's duties towards his fellows those offences made up by the acts which may be undertaken by debauchery. Among these we can particularly distinguish as injurious to the individual's duties towards others *prostitution*, *adultery*, *vices*, *rape* and *sodomy*. Surely we can have no doubt that all so-called moral crimes, that is to say all acts of the type of those which we have just cited, must be of no consequence in a state whose sole duty consists in preserving by whatever means possible the form essential to its maintenance; that is the sole ethic in a republican state.

Since therefore it is always opposed by the despots who surround it, you cannot reasonably imagine its means of maintenance to be *moral means*, for it can maintain itself only by war, and nothing is less moral than war.

Now, I question how one can succeed in proving that in a state obliged to be *immoral* it is essential for the individuals to be *moral*? I will go further – it is good if they are not. The legislators of Greece were perfectly aware of the importance of the need to corrupt its members so that their *moral dissolution* upon that useful to the machine would result in that insurrection which is always indispensable in a government which, completely happy like a republican government, must necessarily excite hatred and jealousy in all who surround it. Insurrection, these wise legislators considered, is by no means a *moral* state; it should be, however, the permanent state of a republic. It would therefore be as absurd as it would be dangerous to demand that those who must maintain the perpetual *immoral* ferment of the machine should themselves be *moral* beings. The reason is that the moral state of a man is one of peace and calm, whereas his immoral state is one of perpetual motion which reconciles him with that necessary insurrection in which the republican must always maintain the government of which he is a member.

Let us now begin our detailed study with an analysis of modesty, this cowardly emotion so opposed to impure attachments. If it had been nature's intention that man should be modest, surely she would not have caused him to be born naked. A multitude of peoples, less degraded than we are by civilization, go naked and experience no shame. There can be no doubt that the use of clothing is based solely upon both the inclemency of the weather, and the coquetry of women; they realized that they would soon lose all the effects of desire if they anticipated them instead of letting them develop; they agreed that in addition nature had not created them without faults, and that they would so much better assure themselves of the means of pleasing by disguising these faults with ornaments. And so modesty, far from being a virtue, was nothing but one of the first effects of corruption, one of the first weapons of female coquetry.

Lycurgus and Solon, in the firm conviction that the results of immodesty maintained the citizen in the immoral state essential to the laws of the republican constitution, obliged young girls to appear naked at the theatres. Rome copied this example; there was dancing in the nude at the Games of Flora. The greatest part of pagan mysteries were celebrated· in this manner; nudity even passed as a virtue among several peoples. Be that as it may, immodesty gives birth to luxurious tastes. The results of these tastes compose the so-called crimes that we are analysing and the first effect of which is prostitution. Now that we have completely turned our backs upon the host of religious errors that enslave us, and in greater intimacy with nature, thanks to the destruction of an army of prejudice, we listen only to her voice, in complete assurance that if anything is criminal it is rather resisting the tastes that she awakes in us than fighting them; in the belief that lust was a consequence of these tastes, we are much less concerned with extinguishing these passions in ourselves than regulating the means of satisfying them in peace. We must therefore apply ourselves to setting up some order in this sphere and establishing in it all the security necessary for the citizen who is impelled by need towards objects of lust to be able to abandon himself with these objects to all that his passions prescribe for him without ever being fettered by anything because there is no passion in man with a greater need for the full extension of liberty than this one. In the towns diverse institutions will be built, healthy, vast, suitably equipped and reliable in every respect. . . . I must explain this still further, measuring it against republican morals. I have promised the same logic throughout, I shall keep my word.

If, as I have just said, no passion has greater need for the full extension of liberty than this one, undoubtedly no other is as despotic. It is in this that man loves to command, to be obeyed, to surround himself with slaves forced to satisfy him. Now every time you fail to give a man the secret means of working off the dose of despotism that nature has placed in the depths of his heart he will turn round and exercise it on the objects which surround him, he will trouble the State. If you wish to avoid this danger, give full scope to these tyrannical desires which despite himself unendingly torment him. Contented by the exercise of his petty sovereignty in the centre of the harem of pashas and sultanas that your cares and his money put at his disposal, he will come away satisfied, with no desire to trouble a government that assures him so complacently every means of satiating his lust. But if, on the contrary, you employ different procedures, if you clutter these objects of public incontinence with all the ridiculous obstacles formerly invented by the tyranny of ministers and the lubricity of our Sardanapales, the man will soon become embittered with the government, jealous of the despotism you impose on him, and weary of your manner of ruling him. Then he will change it, as he has just done.

See how the Greek legislators, imbued with these ideas, dealt with debauchery in Lacedaemonia, in Athens. Far from banning it, they intoxicated the citizen with it. No form of lasciviousness was forbidden him, and Socrates, declared by the oracle to be the wisest of the earth's philosophers, passing indifferently from the arms of Aspasia to those of Alcibiades, was none the less the glory of Greece. I shall go even further, and however contrary my ideas are to our present customs, since it is my aim to prove that we must hurry up and change our customs if we wish to maintain the government we have adopted. . . .

Firstly, by what right do you claim that women should be excepted from that blind submission to the caprices of men which nature prescribed for them and next, by what right do you claim to subject them to a continence that is both physically impossible for them, and of absolutely no value to their honour?

I shall treat each of these questions separately.

It is certain that in the state of nature women are born *vulgivagus*, that is to say enjoying the advantages of other female animals and belonging, like them and without exception, to all males. Such were, without doubt, both the first laws of nature and the only institutions made by the first assemblies of men. *Profit*, *egoism*, and *love* degraded these first designs, such simple and such natural designs. You hoped to get rich by taking a woman and her family's wealth with her – satisfying the first two feelings I have just cited. More often still you carried off this woman and became attached to her; that is the second motive in action, and in every case there is injustice.

An act of possession can never be exercised over a free being. The exclusive possession of a woman is as unjust as the ownership of slaves; all men are born free, all are equal in their rights. Never forget these principles. According to them, therefore, no one sex can ever be granted a legitimate right to take exclusive possession of the other, and one of these sexes or one of these classes can never possess the other arbitrarily. Within the purity of the laws of nature a woman cannot put forward, as a reason for refusing the man who desires her, the love she feels for another, since this reason becomes one of exclusion, and no man can be excluded from possessing a woman, from the moment it is clear that she belongs decisively to all men. The act of possession can be exercised only over a piece of furniture or an animal; it can never be exercised over an individual who resembles us, and all the links which can attach a woman to a man, of any kind you can imagine them to be, are as unjust as they are imaginary.

If therefore it becomes incontestable that we have received from nature the right to express our feelings indiscriminately to all women, in the same way we have the right to oblige each one of them to submit to our wishes, not exclusively, I would assert, but momentarily. It is incontestable that we have the right to establish the laws which force her to give way to the wishes of the man who desires her; since violence even is one of the results of this right, we can use it legally. Well, has not nature proved that we have this right, in giving us the necessary strength to subjugate them to our desires?

In vain do women seek, in their own defence, either modesty or their attachment to other men; these fanciful methods are useless. We have seen earlier that modesty was an artificial and contemptible emotion. Love, which may be called the *madness of the soul*, has no better claim to justify their constancy. It satisfies only two individuals, the lover and the loved; it cannot serve the happiness of others, and it is for the happiness of everyone, not for an egoistic, privileged happiness, that we have been given women.

The 'brochure' that Dolmancé had bought sets out the usual Sadean messages backed up with the usual Sadean examples taken from past civilizations or from the habits of distant countries. All accepted moral systems are reversed: parents are worthless, there is nothing wrong with crime, women should be as promiscuous as men, pregnancy must be avoided, but abortion is available and approved. Nature, and only nature, must be obeyed in all things.

Dolmancé goes out with Augustin, planning deeds so dark that he can describe them to the women only in whispers. Even Eugénie finds them disgusting, and Madame de Saint-Ange's offer of help is declined. 'No, no,' said Dolmancé, 'this is a matter of honour which must take place between men: a woman would disturb us. . . .'

Instead of closing his piece soon after this mysterious move, Sade decided instead to add one of the most revolting incidents he ever described. If so far he had composed not good clean fun but would-be amusing and essentially dirty fun, he chose to reveal Eugénie in a crescendo of depravity. The girl's prudish and worried mother has come to see what has happened to her daughter. The company decide that not only must she be punished for the way she has attempted to bring up Eugénie in total naïvety, but annihilated. There has been non-stop sexuality in the boudoir, as well as 'philosophy', but there has not been serious brutality. Now there is, for a valet suffering from smallpox is ordered to infect Madame de Mistival with the disease through sexual intercourse and it is Eugénie who sews up her vagina to make certain that the contagion will not fail.

Dolmancé announces that he and his three friends will now have dinner and after that: '. . . all four of us in the same bed. This was a good day! I never eat better, I never sleep more peacefully than when I have polluted myself sufficiently during the day with what stupid people call crimes'.

If many readers bought the book in secret, Sade himself was more impoverished than ever, and even when La Coste was sold his possessions were sequestrated. He even confessed to stealing things from one of his sons in order to sell them and buy food. In 1799 he worked for a pittance in the theatre at Versailles. However, his play *Oxtiern* was performed again – as mentioned earlier, he acted in it himself –

and it was published. So were his stories, *Les Crimes de l'Amour*, prefaced by his interesting essay on the novel. Since they were not pornographic they were announced as written 'by the author of *Aline et Valcour*'. The year 1800, despite his poverty, could have made him a reasonably well-known author if not a rich one.

# Histoire Secrète d'Isabelle de Bavière

By the turn of the century Sade had been in principle a free man for six years, even if he had never been free from poverty. In the spring of 1801, the 15th Ventôse, that freedom came to an end, for the First Consul, who had appointed himself in 1799, was trying to restore some degree of decency into the moral chaos of the post-revolutionary period. The police raided Sade's publisher Massé, where he and the author were discussing business. *La Nouvelle Justine* and the last volume of *Juliette* were seized, despite Sade's denial of authorship. At the house of Marie-Constance, who now lived in Saint-Ouen, a tapestry was found with obscene designs based on episodes from *Justine*. The authorities decided to avoid the scandal of a court case and merely incarcerated Sade in the converted convent of Sainte-Pélagie, as an 'administrative punishment'.

He was not ready to accept such a despotic reason for detention. He was ready to stand trial, but was not allowed to do so. He was transferred to the prison of Bicêtre, known by the unenviable title of 'the Bastille for the rabble'. Sade was sixty-one, considered to be old at the time, but at least his family came to his aid, though in a selfish way, for they were not concerned with obtaining his freedom. They asked for him to be sent to Charenton-Saint-Maurice, the hospice for the mad where he had been sent briefly in 1789. They agreed to pay for his keep. Since 1797 Charenton had been placed under the supervision of the Ministère de l'Intérieur, therefore the existence of this particular prisoner-patient would not be forgotten. Marie-Constance, who had naturally pleaded for Sade's release, was eventually allowed to live close to him at Charenton, described, for the sake of *les convenances*, as his daughter or even as his niece.

What now? Sade's talent was for action and aggression, even if these had been restricted for a long time to his writing. Since he could not be idle, he continued to write and was able to return to his love of the theatre by writing and producing plays for the inmates of Charenton. The writer Charles Nodier, who had seen Sade at Bicêtre, wrote a brief description of the man who no doubt looked the same way during his early years at the hospital: he was enormously fat, which prevented him from displaying the last traces of grace and elegance, still discernible in his manners. 'Yet his tired eyes still preserved something of brilliance and finesse which glowed in them from time to time like a dying spark among extinct embers.'

At Charenton Sade's dramatic activities earned him friends and enemies; the patients were occupied, if not cured, and it became a fashionable pastime for many Parisians to see the plays. One doctor who disliked Sade complained that he was causing too much disturbance and hoped, since he was clearly not mad, that he would be transferred to a secure fortress. The director, and Sade's family, prevented any such move.

He never stopped writing, and Marie-Constance would go out into Paris for him, successfully placing some of his plays with various theatres. He wrote at least part of a vast novel, *Les Journées de Florbelle*, which was subsequently destroyed. He also wrote three historical novels, one of which was published in 1813, *La Marquise de Ganges*. This true story seemed ready-made for Sade, for the beautiful young marquise had been killed in 1667 by her two brothers-in-law, one of them an abbé, in a cruel melodrama of love and money which caused a sensation at the time. Sade's last two books were also historical novels, a genre that fascinated him, since he enjoyed the research and liked to point out how past historians had gone wrong. They were also about women: Adelaïde de Brunswick, an early medieval queen, and Isabelle de Bavière, who lived from 1371 to 1435, wife of Charles VI of France, known as the Mad and also as the Good. One of their sons was the Dauphin befriended by Joan of Arc, and their daughter Catherine became the wife of Henry V of England. Although these novels are confused and unimpressive, Isabelle is intriguing because at one level she could even be compared with Juliette. As regent of France, during her husband's phases of madness, she was devious and cruel, aspired to total power and if necessary would have her lovers killed without compunction. Sade obviously enjoyed creating her portrait:

Along with the usual charms and graces of her age Isabelle's features displayed a kind of pride rarely found at the age of sixteen. In her eyes, which were very large and very black, could be seen more pride than the sensitivity so sweet and attractive in the innocent glances of a young person. Her figure indicated loftiness and flexibility, her gestures were firm, her walk was bold, her voice a little harsh, her words few. Much haughtiness in her character, no trace of that tender humanity, the privilege of fine souls which, bringing them nearer to the throne, consoles them for that painful distance at which fate caused them to be born. Dismissive already about morality and the religion which supports it; an insurmountable aversion to everything which opposed her tastes; unyielding in her moods; extreme in her pleasures; a dangerous inclination to vengeance; finding with ease wrongs in those who surrounded her, as quick to suspect as to punish, to produce evil deeds as to contemplate them in cold blood; proving through certain traits that when love inflamed her heart she would yield only to its rages and would see in it only a useful purpose. At the same time avaricious and prodigal, desiring everything, interfering in everything, knowing the value of nothing, cherishing in truth only herself, sacrificing all interests, even those of the State, to her own; gratified by the rank in which fate placed her, not in order to do good, but to find in it the impunity of evil; in fact possessing all the vices unredeemed by a single virtue.

[Isabelle was a version of Juliette, surely, and she had belonged to the world of reality. Sade ended his introduction to the book with an invocation to his last heroine.]

Oh you whom fate called to the support of a throne that was already crumbling, should you then have hastened its fall? But, seduced or rather corrupted by the examples placed before your eyes, do you not have some rights to the indulgence of posterity? Ah, no doubt if you had at least offered us some virtues! But it is in vain that one desires them, it is without success that one seeks them; in you one finds only disorder and it is with frankness that we are going to prove some sad truths which have remained too long unknown, but they must be revealed at last, both for the instruction of all and in order to establish more firmly in our hearts the inviolable devotion and respect that we constantly owe to those of our sovereign queens truly deserving of our praise and our homage. . . .

Sade was claiming that his interest in evil women was due to his search for truth, and his belief that the wickedness of Isabelle (much written about in France, not too well known outside it) would highlight the goodness of others, the Justines as it were of history.

# Journal, 1814

During his years at Charenton, his last years, Sade was not concerned uniquely with history. He continued naturally enough in the hope that he could prove his innocence and his belief in the Republic. But that hope must have grown faint. His two sons, who had not seen him for many years, visited him. The elder, Louis-Marie, had inherited his father's interest in history and in fact wrote a history of France. This young man took part in the Battle of Jena and then sadly he was killed in a skirmish with Neapolitan soldiers in Italy in 1809. The previous year Sade's younger son, Donatien-Claude-Armand, had sought his father's consent for his marriage to a member of the Sade-Eyguières family, a consent which at first he refused. The elderly Charenton patient was not convinced that his son would work for his freedom and preserve his assets. Eventually this marriage took place in 1808 and ensured the continuation of the Sade family until the present day.

Sade's separated wife died in 1810 at the Normandy château of Echauffour and was buried in the same grave as her mother. In the 1950s the inscription on the tomb was still readable: the two women were described as *toutes les deux aussi vertueuses que bienfaisantes*.

Many kilometres away at Charenton the author-patient-prisoner still had the support of Marie-Constance Quesnet, but that did not limit his interest in other women. In 1808 he had noticed a girl of barely twelve who worked at the hospice. Ironically enough she was helping Marie-Constance, who was ill at the time. The girl was called Madeleine Leclerc. She may have been apprenticed either as a seamstress or a laundry-maid, and her mother was on the staff also. As she grew a little older, Sade encouraged her to visit him. He offered to teach her to write and to sing. They became intimate. The Journal he kept in a kind of shorthand has preserved something of the last few years of Sade's life and his fragile relationship with Madeleine Leclerc. This Journal consisted originally of four notebooks. Two have survived and the following extracts are taken from the fourth and last of them.

The few pages need a glossary, a dramatis personae, for Sade, always given to the use of mysterious numbers and code names in his letters, wrote here in a form as abbreviated as possible. In the original Madeleine's name is given as Mgl. Otherwise:

Md.     Madame Quesnet
Md. Lec     Madame Leclerc, Madeleine's mother
La Coulange     presumably a worker at Charenton
Armand     Sade's younger son Donatien-Claude-Armand
Isabelle     Sade's novel *Isabelle de Bavière*
Madame de Saxe     Sade's novel *Adelaïde de Brunswick*
Pigoreau     a bookseller
Bleni (correctly Bleynie)     the assistant chief medical officer
Moïse     Sade himself
Roze     Sade's notary
Φ     sexual intercourse

Many persons named cannot be identified and a few incomprehensible sentences have been omitted.

MONTH OF OCTOBER 1814

On the 2nd, at the time when I was expecting Madeleine, she sent la Coulange with a letter saying that she could come only next Sunday and that she was sending me a good pair of very warm stockings. I replied in some anger. . . .

On the 9th Madeleine made her 91st visit. She behaved very well and said very intelligent things, urged me strongly to calm myself on her account, assuring me that she would never let me down, that even if her mother left the establishment that would not prevent her from coming with me; she urged me not to spend money on her behalf, saying that in the past I spent much less and that had caused me trouble. There was all the more reason why that would cause me a very different kind of trouble today and she said she would give me another pair of rabbit-skin stockings for New Year's Day, and that when we were together she would give me many things that could be useful to me. She added that she was very badly fed, that only 3 francs a week were spent on her and something extra if she stayed the night, and this she told me very wisely meant that she did not want to eat good things which she would miss later. I gave her a little reading and writing lesson; she promised me she would work on it during the long evenings. Moreover I found her progress was not too bad. She said that her health continued to be not good and that in eight or ten days she will consult De Guise if it continued to be bad. . . .

On the 16th Madeleine, who was due to come sent la Coulange with a letter to say that she would come in a week's time, that is to say on the 23rd. La Coulange had told me that Madeleine was prevented from coming because she was working with la Blénie. That was false, she had gone out walking with her mother.

On the 17th Madame was leaving for Paris and was not due to return until the next day. She said strange things when she came to say goodbye to me; her remarks were absurd. She took away *La Tour Mystérieuse* and *Les Jumelles* with her in order to place them.

Madame came back from Paris on the 18th at dinner-time, she had placed the two plays, one at the Odéon, the other with Fedeau; but she had seen Vaillant who had told her that the police had written to my family asking them to take me away. They had replied that they did not want to do so and that it was Monsieur Cole, secretary to the director of police, who had written and who had received the reply that the family did not want this. In addition she brought back the monthly allowance along with the wood and said that Boursier will come to see me towards the end of the month.

The same day Madame Leclerc who was due to come on Friday 21st had me informed that she would come only on the 24th.

On the 23rd I was waiting for her [Madeleine] at the usual time. At ten o'clock la Coulange came to tell me that she would come at only eleven o'clock or twelve. She came at a quarter past twelve and stayed until two o'clock, remained cold, and when I reproached her for it she told me that it was the fault of the establishment and that she would be quite different outside. She promised me sincerely to remain faithful and attached to me and that I could count on her, she was having her period. She gave the best possible reasons for the impossibility of breakfasts and I accepted them. In the course of all that she uttered many unkind remarks and even gave me to understand that the regulations would not allow me to leave, and that she would be dismissed, that we should be very careful about this, she took 10 (fr.) for a new waistcoat, for which she would be responsible, as well as two pairs of stockings. In spite of everything there was thought of Φ for a moment and it was promised for next Sunday. She reasoned perfectly well about mistresses or lovers who published abroad the favours they received and protested to me that she had never committed any indiscretion on this subject.

On the 24th I expected her mother who had promised to come and did not come. But it wasn't her fault. The same day Quesnet had been robbed and the two serving women were suspected.

On the 26th the mother, having had me informed of her visit, came at one o'clock and promised with an air of frankness and truth that our plans would not change in any way. She asked me what I would do, I explained things to her. As for M . . . [Madeleine] she asked if I had spoken to her daughter about it. I said that yes, I had. She asked me how she had replied. In the affirmative, I answered. Well then, she said, how could I not consent to it after that? She showed the strongest desire to see her daughter happy and said on this topic that she would prefer her simply to serve me, rather than do anything else. I said all that one can say on that subject and in the end I was satisfied. She told me that she believed Varenne to be stupid rather than subtle and spiteful, etc. . . . It was said that the payment had arrived.

On the 30th Madeleine came as she had promised to make her 93rd visit. She stayed two hours: she had arrived at eight and did not leave until after ten. She was very amiable, promised to care for me in an astonishing way when we were together, she drank, wrote and sang, said that she was going to be better fed and that she was very pleased with her mother, that she was taking eau-de-Cologne and sugar for her stomach and that it was doing her good; she appeared to be wonderfully well, she brought me a pair of stockings etc. . . .

## MONTH OF NOVEMBER

On the 5th in the evening Madame went to see the director who was extremely anxious that I should write to my son asking him to pay the arrears. He refused permission outright for Donge to read the newspaper to me and the next day I wrote to him asking that this Donge might at least continue to do his copying.

Moreover Madame was pleased with what he said about me and all that seemed to me to go fairly well, apart from the refusal of the reading. . . .

On the 6th Madeleine came to make her 94th visit. She came at nine o'clock and was in good form, she even appeared intelligent, but made me see that despite the submissiveness she had sworn to me there were two things she would not do and I saw in general that in all this she would do only what she wanted to do. She continued to be inactive and careless and even cold during the session. I can give her only *une figure*. She was satisfied by that and made delicate remarks on the subject. She brought me a pair of stockings. . . .

On the 10th I saw the director in the evening, I was very pleased by this. On the same day Paquet at my request brought Isabelle for the corrections. . . .

On the 13th I was waiting for Madeleine, Madame paid a surprise visit. She stayed for a quarter of an hour. I continued to wait for Madeleine.

On the 13th the director gave a big dinner-party, to which we were not invited. On the same day Madeleine, who was expected, did not come and Madame came to make a scene, thinking that she was there.

On the 14th Madeleine let it be known that she would come on Sunday the 20th.

On the 17th I was told that a commission was going to come. On this same day Madame is going to Paris for the money.

On her return from Paris we had a few arguments with Madame but it was I who was mistaken. Madame announced a visit from her mother-in-law on Monday the 21st.

On the 20th Madeleine, who had promised to choose the

time of mass, enjoyed herself over breakfast and instead of coming at nine o'clock as she had promised came only at a quarter past ten. She was having her period, was very good in conversation but uncaring about pleasure, talked about being a housekeeper, said she didn't want to eat either in the kitchen or with the cook. She had not practised her writing, which annoyed me, but she read not badly.

I told her as was true that my health had not been good for a fortnight. She appeared to be sorry about it, promised to come back on Sunday the 27th and wanted some chocolate. She said there would be two balls here, one on St Catherine's day the other on St Nicholas's day, to which she would not go because she knew that would please me. I thanked her for that.

On the 21st my cousin came to make her 8th visit. I was very pleased with her. She understood very well how I was suffering and said in a very sensitive way that if they didn't prescribe old wine for me she would send some herself, that the family had definitely decided to pay the extra expenses of this treatment, but she urged that the room should be changed. She went to see the director, to whom she told all this, and the next day Bleni came to see me and prescribed the treatment which I adopted and which I shall follow.

My cousin spoke several times about freedom.

On the 22nd I saw Bleni. He gave me a prescription. At first they provided the old wine and the next day they only gave two quarter bottles and the treatment was completely upset. Madame went to complain on my behalf.

Madame went quickly to Paris in order to find 78 francs.

The same day, the 26th, Madame came back from Paris and brought the money but no wine. She said that Boursier was waiting for his money. My pains were still very severe. The under-doctor came to apply the suspensory bandage. By this day I'd been in pain for a week, especially when touched or in the evenings.

On the 27th Madeleine came to make her 96th visit. She seemed very sympathetic about my pains, which I described to her. She had not been to any balls and promised to go to none, spoke of the future, said that she would be eighteen on the 19th of next month, thanked me for what I was doing for her and made it clear that she was neither deceiving nor wished to deceive. During this visit Varenne brought the reply from Monsieur Roze, who was going to set things in motion. Madeleine stayed for two hours and I was very pleased.

Madeleine: during her visit, all the libertinage of the balls described by Rousseau.

Madame assured Moïse that, from all her mother-in-law had said, it was impossible to rely on anything before the spring. Which as I see it should take until 5th or 6th March, making fourteen years in all and eleven years five or six days, the figure marked in pencil on my door at Pélagie.

On 30th November 1814 they placed the leather truss on me for the first time. . . .

These are probably among the last words written by Sade.

# Testament

Neither the flighty Madeleine Leclerc nor Marie-Constance Quesnet was with Sade during the last few hours of his life. But the old man did not die alone. His son Donatien-Claude-Armand had been given permission to visit him on 2nd December 1814 and, obviously concerned about the state of his father's health, asked L.-J. Ramon, the junior house doctor, who was only nineteen and still a student, to spend the night with him. Although this was not one of his normal duties, he carried it out, arriving just as the Charenton priest was leaving. Ramon gave the patient a few mouthfuls of herbal tea from time to time and a dose of the medicine prescribed for his breathing difficulties. Soon afterwards, at about 10 p.m., the Marquis de Sade died in uncomplaining silence.

He had made his will in 1806. Three years later he told his son, whose views were puritanical, not to complain about his perpetual scribbling. 'Don't be sorry', he said, 'to see your name immortalized: my works will bring this about, and your virtues, although preferable to my works, would never have done so.'

The greater part of his will proved Sade's generous recognition of Marie-Constance Quesnet, for he left her virtually everything. His executor received a valuable ring and his family received only the papers Sade himself had inherited from his father in 1767. In the fifth and last part of his will, however, Sade seemed anxious to be forgotten by the whole world:

I forbid my body to be opened under any pretext whatsoever. I demand with the greatest insistence that it should be kept forty-eight hours in the room where I shall die, placed in a wooden coffin which will be nailed down only after the forty-eight hours referred to above, on the expiration of which the said coffin will be closed; during this time a dispatch shall be sent to the Sieur Lenormand, wood merchant, boulevard l'Egalité No. 101 at Versailles, asking him to come himself together with a wagon to take my body in order to transport it under his escort to the wood on my estate at Malmaison in the province of Mance near Epernon where I want it to be placed without any form of ceremony in the first overgrown thicket which is found on the right in the said wood as you come into it on the side of the old castle by the wide alley which divides the wood in two. My grave shall be dug in this thicket by the farmer of Malmaison under the inspection of Monsieur Lenormand, who shall not leave my body before it has been placed in the said grave. He can be accompanied during the ceremony, if he wishes, by those among my relatives or friends who without any show of mourning will want to give me this last sign of attachment. Once the grave has been filled in it shall be sown over with acorns so that afterwards the ground of the said grave having been replanted and the thicket being overgrown as it was before, the traces of my tomb will disappear from the surface of the earth, as I flatter myself that my memory will be effaced from the minds of men, except none the less from those of the small number of people who have been pleased to love me up to the last moment and of whom I carry into the grave a most tender recollection.

Made at Charenton-Saint-Maurice when of sound mind and in good health, January 30th, 1806.

*signed* D.A.F. Sade

If Sade's son had various virtues they are not easily seen, and a wish to preserve his father's literary work was not one of them. He asked the police authorities to destroy the manuscript of *Les Journées de Florbelle*, which had been left incomplete, and was even present to watch the pages crumple and vanish in the flames. Only outline notes remain of what was to have been a vast novel. Twenty years or so after his father's death he was still ready to repeat an earlier request to the editor of the *Biographie Michaud*: he asked for the name of his father, 'accused of being the author of the infamous *Justine*', not to be included. He made this request because of 'my name, my numerous family and my misfortunes'. The request was not granted.

Sade once remarked that 'the entr'actes in my life have been too long'. At the end of the twentieth century, as previously unknown works by this unique writer are discovered or reprinted, and as public taste and behaviour change, he is still speaking the epilogue.

# Chronology

| | |
|---|---|
| 1740 | At the Hôtel de Condé, Paris, on 2nd June, birth of Donatien-Alphonse-François de Sade, only surviving child of the Comte and Comtesse de Sade. |
| 1744–50 | Education in Provence, directed by his uncle, the Abbé de Sade. |
| 1750 | Education in Paris at the Jesuit Collège Louis-le-Grand, and by private tutor. |
| 1754 | Enters cavalry school, L'Ecole des Chevau-légers, to which only members of old aristocratic families were admitted. |
| 1755 | Commissioned as sub-lieutenant in the King's infantry regiment. |
| 1756 | Outbreak of Seven Years War. |
| 1757 | Made cornet in the Carabinier regiment of the Comte de Provence. |
| 1759 | Becomes a captain in the cavalry regiment of Bourgogne. |
| 1763 | Demobilized at the end of the Seven Years War. Marriage (mid-May) to Renée-Pélagie de Montreuil. Imprisonment (late October) for two weeks following excessive debauchery and impiety. |
| 1764 | Replaces his father as Lieutenant-General of Bresse, Bugey, Valromey and Gex. |
| 1764–6 | Liaisons with actresses, including Mesdemoiselles Colet and de Beauvoisin. |
| 1767 | Death of his father (January). Birth of his first son, Louis-Marie (August). |
| 1768 | The flagellation of Rose Keller (April), leading to imprisonment for two weeks at Saumur and Pierre-Encise. Released in November. |

| 1769 | Birth of his second son, Donatien-Claude-Armand. |
| 1771 | Birth of his daughter, Madeleine-Laure. Imprisonment for debt. Love affair with his wife's sister, Anne-Prospère. |
| 1772 | 'Affair of the poisoned sweets' in Marseille, leading to charges of poisoning and sodomy. Sentenced to death in Aix, during flight to Italy with Anne-Prospère. Arrested in Chambéry and imprisoned at Miolans. |
| 1773 | Escapes from prison and returns to the family château of La Coste near Avignon. |
| 1775 | Sexual orgies with young girls at the château. Second flight to Italy. |
| 1776 | Returns to La Coste. |
| 1777 | Death of his mother. He is arrested in Paris and imprisoned at Vincennes. |
| 1778 | Authorized to travel to Aix, where his earlier death sentence was quashed, although he was admonished for 'exaggerated debauchery'. Escapes on his way back to prison but is recaptured at La Coste. |
| 1781 | After three years his wife is allowed to visit him. |
| 1782 | Finishes writing the *Dialogue entre un Prêtre et un Moribond* and begins *Les Cent Vingt Journées de Sodome*. |
| 1784 | Transferred to the Bastille. |
| 1785 | Transcribes *Les Cent Vingt Journées* on to long roll of paper. |
| 1786–7 | Starts to write *Aline et Valcour* and also short stories. |
| 1789 | Shouts to the crowd from his window at the Bastille. Transferred to Charenton-Saint-Maurice. |
| 1790 | Released from Charenton. Separation from his wife, followed by relationship with Marie-Constance Quesnet. |
| 1791 | Clandestine publication of *Justine, ou Les Malheurs de la Vertu*. Performance of his play *Le Comte Oxtiern*. |
| 1791 | Made secretary of the Section des Piques. Vandalization of the Château de La Coste. |
| 1792 | *Aline et Valcour* published. |
| 1793 | Arrested on suspicion of support for the *ancien régime*. |
| 1794 | Imprisoned, condemned to death but later released after Thermidor. |
| 1795 | Publication of *La Philosophie dans le Boudoir*, announced as a posthumous work by the author of *Justine*. *Aline et Valcour* published openly. |

1796    Château de La Coste sold.

1797    Probable publication, anonymously, of *La Nouvelle Justine*, followed by *L'Histoire de Juliette*.

1799    *Oxtiern* performed again, Sade acting a part in it.

1800    *Oxtiern* and *Les Crimes de l'Amour* published.

1801    Arrested on the premises of his publisher. An edition of *Justine* and *Juliette* seized. Imprisonment in Sainte-Pélagie and Bicêtre.

1803    Transfer to Charenton.

1807    Writes *Les Journées de Florbelle*. Manuscripts in his room are seized.

1808    Marriage of his younger son Donatien-Claude-Armand

1809    Death of his elder son, Louis-Marie, in Italy.

1810    Death of his separated wife.

1813    Publication of *La Marquise de Ganges*.

1814    Death of Sade, 2nd December.

(Based in part on the chronology included in each volume of the *Oeuvres Complètes*, Pauvert, Paris, 1986– .)

# Bibliography

In December 1956 the 17th Correctional Chamber of Paris heard a case brought by Le Ministère Publique (the State Prosecutor) against the publishing firm Les Editions Jean-Jacques Pauvert for having published works by Sade 'contraires aux bonnes moeurs'. The publishers were defended by the eminent lawyer Maître Maurice Garçon and evidence on their behalf was supplied by four leading writers – Jean Paulhan, Georges Bataille, Jean Cocteau and André Breton.

In a letter Cocteau wrote: 'The least important detective novel from prudish America is more pernicious than the most audacious page by Sade.' Ironically, the submission by André Breton, the surrealist leader, 'unfortunately went astray and could not be read during the session'. He began his statement by quoting Sade's own self-defence: 'I speak only to those capable of understanding me, and they will read me without danger.'

The judgement delivered the following month ordered that the titles incriminated (Sade's four major works) were to be confiscated and destroyed. The publishers were fined and ordered to pay costs. They appealed but the judgement was upheld.

A short transcript of the hearing had been published by Pauvert in 1957 before the appeal was heard. In 1987 the same publishers, with a new imprint, began to issue the complete works in a series, to date, of fifteen volumes. Three years later the first volume of Sade's complete writing appeared in the Bibliothèque de la Pléiade, the series of works which includes only those deemed to have 'classic' status.

During 1966–7 Sade's *Oeuvres Complètes* were published in sixteen volumes by Le Cercle du Livre Précieux, Paris.

From 1986 onwards a new edition of the *Oeuvres Complètes*,

established by Annie Le Brun and Jean-Jacques Pauvert, has been published by the Société Nouvelle des Editions Pauvert, in fifteen volumes to date (1991).

On 23rd May 1986 the Paris newspaper *Libération* published a supplement devoted to Sade, including the latest literary and critical developments to date, news of ongoing research directed by his descendant Thibault de Sade, and a previously unpublished poem (1947) about the writer, entitled *Le Prisonnier*, by the Mexican poet Octavio Paz.

Forthcoming publications, edited by Maurice Lever and Thibault de Sade, are expected to include 'plays, poems, stories, moral works and letters so far unpublished'.

## SOME POSTHUMOUS PUBLICATIONS

1904 *Les 120 Journées de Sodome*. Ed. Dr Eugen Dühren. Club des Bibliophiles, Paris. 180 copies. (Publication was in fact in Berlin, Max Harrwitz)

1909 *L'Oeuvre du Marquis de Sade*, pages choisies. Introduction, essai bibliographique et notes par Guillaume Apollinaire. Bibliothèque des Curieux, Paris

1926 *Historiettes, Contes et Fabliaux*. Inédits publiés par Maurice Heine, pour les membres de la Société du roman philosophique. Paris

1926 *Dialogue entre un Prêtre et un Moribond*. Avant-propos et des notes par Maurice Heine. Stendhal et Compagnie, Paris

1930 *Les Infortunes de la Vertu*. Introduction par Maurice Heine. Editions Fourcade, Paris

1949 *L'Aigle, Mademoiselle* . . . Préface et commentaire par Gilbert Lély. Les Editions Georges Artigues, Paris

1953 *Histoire Secrète d'Isabelle de Bavière, Reine de France*. Avant-propos par Gilbert Lély. Gallimard, Paris

1954 *Adelaide of Brunswick*. Translated by Professor Hobart Ryland, Scarecrow Press, Washington, DC

1963 *Lettres Choisies*. Préface par Gilbert Lély. Pauvert, Paris

1970 *Journal Inédit*. Deux cahiers retrouvés du journal inédit du Marquis de Sade, 1807–1808, 1814, ed. Georges Daumas. Gallimard, Paris

## SELECTED BIOGRAPHICAL AND CRITICAL WORKS

Apollinaire, Guillaume. *Les Diables Amoureux*. Gallimard, Paris, 1964

Beauvoir, Simone de. *Faut-il Brûler Sade?* Gallimard, Paris, 1955

Bloch, Dr Iwan. *Marquis de Sade*. Brittany Press, USA, 1948 ed.

Carter, Angela. *The Sadeian Woman*. Virago, London, 1979

Gorer, Geoffrey. *The Life and Ideas of the Marquis de Sade* (enlarged and revised edition). Peter Owen, London, 1953

Hayman, Ronald. *De Sade, a Critical Biography*. Constable, London, 1978

Lély, Gilbert. *Vie du Marquis de Sade*. 2 vols, Gallimard, Paris, 1952–7

Pauvert, Jean-Jacques (ed.). *L'Affaire Sade*. Pauvert, Paris, 1957 (1000 numbered copies)


## OTHER

Bloch, Robert. *The Skull of the Marquis de Sade* (fiction). Pyramid Publications, New York, 1965

Breton, André (ed.). *Anthologie de l'Humour Noir*, Pauvert, Paris, 1966

Camus, Albert. *L'Homme Revolté*. Gallimard, Paris, 1951

Delpech, Jeannine. *La Passion de la Marquise de Sade*. Editions Planète, Paris, 1970

Hyde, H. Montgomery. *A History of Pornography*. Heinemann, London, 1964

Mishima, Yukio. *Madame de Sade* (play). Peter Owen, London, 1968

Praz, Mario. *The Romantic Agony*. OUP, Oxford, 2nd ed. 1951

Weiss, Peter. *Marat/Sade* (short title) (play). Suhrkamp, Frankfurt-am-Main, W. Germany, 1964

MICHEL TOURNIER

# Four Wise Men

The legend of the Magi is one of the most potent episodes in the Christian tradition. This dazzling novel performs the feat of bringing them to life – Gaspard, Melchior and Balthasar, each in quest of what he loved most, and has lost.

    But Tournier departs from the Bible story with his unforgettable addition of the fourth King – Taor, the one who came too late for the Nativity.

'Imaginative, macabre and dreamlike'
    Graham Lord, *Sunday Express*

'Enthralling . . . a beguiling work of art'
    Paul Bailey, *Standard*

'A true masterpiece'
    *New Statesman*

'Dazzling . . . intriguing'
    John Weightman, *Observer*

'An astonishing elaboration of the Epiphany legend . . . The most peculiarly inventive novel of the year'
    Victoria Glendinning, *Sunday Times*

MICHEL TOURNIER

# The Fetishist

Subversive, funny, disturbing, the stories in this volume range from familiar figures of myth – Adam, Father Christmas – to mundane lorry drivers and murderous dwarves, but all display Michel Tournier's dazzling imagination and ferocious vitality. His adult fables explore a world of mysterious sexuality and re-interpreted legend, and further confirm his status as one of Europe's greatest living writers.

'The most gifted and original novelist to emerge in France since the war'
*Observer*

'Mr Tournier is a disturbing virtuoso. His technical range is stunning. His prose is sensuous and muscular; it can be colloquial, stylised, restrained, exuberant. Tones shift as he quickly moves from realism to irony, from the whimsical to the violently preposterous . . . the stories he writes are fairytales for adults only'
*New York Times*

'*a danse macabre*, spotlit by surrealism . . . A fascinating box of conjuring tricks'
*Financial Times*

MICHEL TOURNIER

# The Midnight Love Feast

'The fables in Tournier's *The Midnight Love Feast* are told by guests invited to a divorce binge thrown by an ill-matched couple . . . What every story reveals is the astonishing resourcefulness of Tournier's imagination. They constitute the purest literature, arrestingly simple ideas planted in the fertile sod of a storyteller's brain'
Jasper Rees, *The Times*

'The 19 tales – some realist, some fabulist; some of them fully rounded narratives, others brief, perfunctory musings – contextualise the problems of a couple falling out of love with one another. Tournier's writing has a direct beauty and a delightful metaphorical grace; he's got the sagacity of a Primo Levi and the supple inventiveness of a Gabriel Garcia Marquez'
James Saynor, *Observer*

'Tournier has cast his spell. He writes with economy and imagination, always standing back from the action; yet always present in the reader's mind, eager to share his own pleasure in language and his sense of fun . . . What is outstanding – and this is something that only an excellent translation could effect – is not its cleverness but its clarity, its ability to say "once upon a time"'
Judy Cooke, *Guardian*

LAWRENCE NORFOLK

# Lemprière's Dictionary

'What serpentine narration secretly connects
the founding of the East India Company in
1600, a massacre of innocents at the siege of La
Rochelle 27 years later, and the publication of
Lemprière's celebrated classical dictionary on
the eve of the French Revolution? The answer
is this ingeniously contrived, spellbinding fable.
An extraordinary first novel'
    *City Limits*

'It's poised, superbly inventive and . . .
gripping. With *Lemprière's Dictionary* the
precocious author has catapulted himself into
the premier league of English fiction writing'
    *Observer*

'An extraordinary achievement . . . at once a
quest, a tragedy, a political thriller and a
cultural meditation. It is a remarkable book'
    *Times Literary Supplement*

'This is historical fiction of mesmerising
complexity . . . It is a masterpiece'
    *Daily Mail*

'A love story, and a story of fantastic
adventure, it is also a hugely comic novel . . .
immense verve and brilliance'
    *Sunday Times*

FRANZ KAFKA

# The Complete Short Stories

This volume contains all of Kafka's shorter
fiction, from fragments, parables and sketches
to longer, complete tales. Together they reveal
the breadth of Kafka's literary vision and the
extraordinary imaginative depth of his thought.
Some – like *The Metamorphosis*, in which Gregor
Samsa wakes up to find himself transformed
into a giant insect, or *The Judgement*, written in a
single night of frenzied creativity – are well
known. Others are mere jottings, observations
of daily life, given cameo-like artistic form
through Kafka's unique, idiosyncratic
perception of the world.

Enigmatic and paradoxical, highly personal
but implying the possibility (although never the
attainment) of truths, these pieces of fiction
represent Kafka at his most profoundly
pessimistic and his most whimsically humorous.

'Kafka is important to us because his
predicament is the predicament of modern man'
    W.H. Auden

NICHOLAS MOSLEY

# **Hopeful Monsters**

'Quite simply, the best English novel to have
been written since the Second World War'
A.N. Wilson, *Evening Standard*

'This is a major novel by any standard of
measurement. Its ambition is lofty, its
intelligence startling, and its sympathy
profound. It is frequently funny, sometimes
painful, sometimes moving. It asks
fundamental questions about the nature of
experience . . . It is a novel which makes the
greater part of contemporary fiction seem
pygmy in comparison'
Allan Massie, *The Scotsman*

'Enormously ambitious and continuously
fascinating . . . There is an intellectual
engagement here, a devouring determination to
investigate, to refrain from judgement while
never abandoning moral conventions, that is
rare among British novelists – for that matter,
among novelists of any nationality'
Paul Binding, *New Statesman and Society*

'Nicholas Mosley, in a country never generous
to experimental writing, is one of the more
significant instances we have that it can still,
brilliantly, be done'
Malcolm Bradbury

# The Minerva Anthology of 20th Century Women's Fiction

*Edited by* Judy Cooke

'Judy Cooke's anthology balances the seriousness of its aim – to encapsulate the best in 20th-century women's writing – with a lively eclecticism. In the more than thirty novel extracts and short stories included here, there's a nicely judged mixture of classic texts and new writing, of mainstream and avant-garde. Rosamund Lehmann – but also Angela Carter; Iris Murdoch – but also Marguerite Duras . . .

'Even the familiar stuff gets a fresh look through being seen in a different context – Fay Weldon providing, as it were, an ironic commentary on Virginia Woolf. And was it mere coincidence or something more deliberate which placed Jeanette Winterson's *Sexing the Cherry* after Edith Wharton's *Pomegranate Seed*? Definitely one to pack for the desert island'
       Christina Koning, *Guardian*

'An easy introduction that tantalises and encourages the reader to seek out the full-length originals for her- (or even him-) self'
       Anne Smith, *Scotland on Sunday*

HERBERT ROSENDORFER

# The Night of the Amazons

'*The Night of the Amazons* is a picaresque fantasy
about one Christian Weber, who rises from
being a bouncer in a Munich bar to becoming
regional President, largely as a result of having
a hold over Adolf Hitler. His presidency is
enlivened by the 'Nights of the Amazons', crazy
Wagnerian pageants in which legions of girls
ride on horseback through the streets, wearing
only cardboard helmets and sandals. . . .
Rosendorfer has a flair for extravagant comedy
. . . It would be difficult for anyone to begin this
book without feeling impelled to finish it'
    Robert Nye, *Guardian*

'Herbert Rosendorfer has composed the
blackest of comedies, a brilliantly sustained
piece of invective, charting the career of
Christian Weber, coward, glutton, opportunist,
SS bully boy and 'heroic opponent of the
plutocratic-Communist Jewish conspiracy',
who, while amassing millions for himself
through black-marketeering, monopolies and
confiscations, ends up as City Councillor of
Munich and President of the Kreistag. . . .
Rosendorfer's wit is unrelenting, he spits nails,
aims sledgehammer blows, combining fact and
fiction in a bitter, sweeping, quite deadly satire.
If not every word of *The Night of the Amazons* is
true, it ought to be'
    *Daily Telegraph*

'Raucously funny . . . this is grotesque comedy
at its sharpest'
    *Irish Times*

# A Selected List of Titles Available from Minerva

While every effort is made to keep prices low, it is sometimes necessary to increase prices at short notice. Mandarin Paperbacks reserves the right to show new retail prices on covers which may differ from those previously advertised in the text or elsewhere.

The prices shown below were correct at the time of going to press.

| | | | | |
|---|---|---|---|---|
| ☐ | 7493 9137 5 | **On the Eve of Uncertain Tomorrows** | Neil Bissoondath | £5.99 |
| ☐ | 7493 9050 6 | **Women In A River Landscape** | Heinrich Boll | £4.99 |
| ☐ | 7493 9921 X | **An Instant in the Wind** | Andre Brink | £5.99 |
| ☐ | 7493 9147 2 | **Explosion in a Cathedral** | Alejo Carpentier | £5.99 |
| ☐ | 7493 9109 X | **Bodies of Water** | Michelle Cliff | £4.99 |
| ☐ | 7493 9060 3 | **Century of the Wind** | Eduardo Galeano | £4.99 |
| ☐ | 7493 9080 8 | **Balzacs Horse** | Gert Hofmann | £4.99 |
| ☐ | 7493 9093 X | **The Notebook** | Agota Kristof | £4.99 |
| ☐ | 7493 9174 X | **The Mirror Maker** | Primo Levi | £4.99 |
| ☐ | 7493 9143 X | **Parents Worry** | Gerard Reve | £4.99 |
| ☐ | 7493 9172 3 | **Lives of the Saints** | Nino Ricci | £4.99 |
| ☐ | 7493 9003 4 | **The Fall of the Imam** | Nawal El Saadawi | £4.99 |
| ☐ | 7493 9924 4 | **Ake** | Wole Soyinka | £5.99 |
| ☐ | 7493 9139 1 | **The Four Wise Men** | Michel Tournier | £5.99 |
| ☐ | 7493 9092 1 | **Woman's Decameron** | Julia Voznesenskaya | £5.99 |

All these books are available at your bookshop or newsagent, or can be ordered direct from the publisher. Just tick the titles you want and fill in the form below.

**Mandarin Paperbacks**, Cash Sales Department, PO Box 11, Falmouth, Cornwall TR10 9EN.

Please send cheque or postal order, no currency, for purchase price quoted and allow the following for postage and packing:

| | |
|---|---|
| UK including BFPO | £1.00 for the first book, 50p for the second and 30p for each additional book ordered to a maximum charge of £3.00. |
| Overseas including Eire | £2 for the first book, £1.00 for the second and 50p for each additional book thereafter. |

NAME (Block letters) ..............................................................................................................................

ADDRESS ...............................................................................................................................................

......................................................................................................................................................................

☐ I enclose my remittance for ........................

☐ I wish to pay by Access/Visa Card Number

Expiry Date